KINSHIP WITH ALL LIFE

KINSHIP WITH ALL LIFE By

J. ALLEN BOONE

Author of *Letters to Strongheart* and
You Are the Adventure

1817

Harper & Row, Publishers, San Francisco

New York, Grand Rapids, Philadelphia, St. Louis
London, Singapore, Sydney, Tokyo, Toronto

To the Puccinellis

CONTENTS

CONTENTS

FOREWORD

As we live through these kaleidoscopic days when
confusion, distrust, conflict and misery are so common
everywhere, it is revealing to note that more and more
people are finding reassurance and peace of mind in
companionship beyond the boundaries of humanity.
They are making friends not only with such conventional
favorites as dogs, horses, cats and birds, but with wild
animals, snakes and insects.

Men and women everywhere are being made acutely
aware of the fact that something essential to life and
well-being is flickering very low in the human species
and threatening to go out entirely. This "something" has
to do with such values as love . . . unselfishness . . . integrity . . . sincerity . . . loyalty to one's best . . . honesty . . .
enthusiasm . . . humility . . . goodness . . . happiness
. . . fun. Practically every animal still has these assets in
abundance and is eager to share them, given opportunity
and encouragement.

In this connection it is interesting to recall that people
of certain ancient times appear to have been great virtu-
osos in the art of living, particularly skilled in the delicate
science of being in right relations with everything, in-

cluding animals. These people recognized the inseparable unity of Creator and creation. They were able to blend themselves with the universal Presence, Power and Purpose that is forever moving back of all things, in all things, and through all things. Life to these ancients was an all-inclusive kinship in which nothing was meaningless, nothing unimportant, and from which nothing could be excluded. They refused to make any separating barriers between mineral and vegetable, between vegetable and man, or between man and the great Primal Cause which animates and governs all things. Every living thing was seen as a partner in a universal enterprise. Each had an individual contribution to make to the general good which it, and it alone, could supply. Everything lived for everything else, at all times and under all circumstances.

Those were the days when "the whole earth was of one language and speech . . . and all was one grand concord." Humans, animals, snakes, birds, insects—all shared a common language. By means of this language all were able to express their thoughts and feelings freely on matters of mutual interest. From out of divinely bestowed wisdom, they could reason together for the common good, the common happiness, and the common fun. Evidently this was so simple and natural a part of everyday living as not to need explaining any more than breathing. However one may regard this ancient relationship phenomena, there is evidence that at one time on earth every living thing was able to be in rational correspondence with everything else. Humans and animals moved in full accord not only with one another but with the cosmic Plan as well.

Can we "modern humans" recapture this seemingly lost universal language? Can we by means of it learn to move in genuine good fellowship not only with the members of our own species but with other creatures? I believe that we can. In support of this faith, I have set down in the following pages the true stories of a number of unconventional relationships with animals, reptiles, insects, and even bacteria. None of these adventures was planned or expected. They came into experience as part of the gracious unfoldment of life itself. I begin with the story of the all-time great motion picture dog-star, Strongheart.

As you read these stories you will see that whenever I was properly humble and willing to let something besides a human be my instructor, these various four-legged, six-legged and no-legged fellows shared priceless wisdom with me. They taught me that perfect under-standing and perfect co-operation between the human and all other forms of life is unfailing whenever the human really does his required part.

This has so enriched and broadened my life, has opened up such fascinating new regions to explore and enjoy, that I feel obligated to share at least some of my joy with others.

J. ALLEN BOONE

Hollywood, California

KINSHIP WITH ALL LIFE

1. *FOUR-LEGGED METEOR*

OF all the impacts made on the colorful world of entertainment, few have surpassed that effected by the fabulous German shepherd dog Strongheart. Sweeping suddenly into public notice like a meteor, he became Hollywood's top-ranking screen star and its biggest box-office attraction. For over three years he was the most admired and most loved object above the motion picture horizon. Then with the continuing sweep of a meteor he disappeared from the earth scene and human visibility, leaving millions of men, women and children admirers in all parts of the world.

If you were fortunate enough to have seen Strongheart in some of his films, the mere mention of his name is sure to bring fond recollections. You recall a big, magnificently built dog who did almost incredible things and did them with an intelligence and ease that baffled conventional explanation. If you never saw him in the movies, he is still well worth knowing because of the great things he continues to share across time, space and the phenomenon of death itself.

Strongheart came to Hollywood as the result of an idea on the part of two widely known entertainment-creating personalities: Jane Murfin, a distinguished writer of stage and screen plays, and Larry Trimble, a producer and director. Larry was in a class all by himself when it came to understanding wild and domestic animals and persuading them to work for him in front of motion-picture cameras. Jane and Larry's idea was to search the world for an unusual dog, bring him to Hollywood and star him in a series of special dramatic films. Dogs had been used before as "bit players" in screen stories, but this was the first time that a dog was to be given the leading role in a major production and top billing in all advertising and publicity.

The dog they finally decided upon, because of his looks, size, background and accomplishments, was Strongheart, whose kennel name in Germany had been Etzel von Oerengen. Strongheart came from a long line of carefully bred, highly efficient, blue-ribboned shepherd dogs, all of which had won their awards not only for the finest in physical appearance but also for their ability to qualify as work, police and war dogs. Strongheart's father was the international champion Nores, and the only dog that was ever able to beat him in open competition was Strongheart.

Strongheart was a dogman's dream of a dog, having in perfection all the qualities that a dog of his type is supposed to have. He was powerfully built, unusually capable and utterly fearless. His weight fluctuated between 115 and 125 pounds, yet he moved with amazing speed and agility. He had to in order to accomplish what he did in military and police work.

And so to Hollywood to try his luck in the movies

came this big German shepherd, a famous champion in his own country but practically unknown on this side of the Atlantic except to the relatively few who for professional reasons kept a watchful eye on dog show winners throughout the world. Strongheart crossed the United States from New York to Los Angeles as just another dog in the baggage car. There was no one of importance to greet him when he arrived, no reporters, no cameramen. Without ceremony he was removed from the baggage car, placed in quite an ordinary automobile and taken to a Hollywood studio where screen tests of him were to be made. None of the members of the film colony knew that he was coming, and if they had it would have created little interest; dogs for movie purposes at that time were a dime a dozen.

A little over a year later Strongheart was again placed on a train, but this time he did not have to ride in the baggage car. Instead, he was escorted with all possible honors through lanes of excited admirers and placed in a special suite aboard the best train out of Los Angeles. He was attended by a manager, a valet, a press-agent, and a special representative of the railroad who was there to see that he got the best, and only the best, of everything.

By nation-wide demand Strongheart was making a personal appearance tour of the country. From coast to coast, newspapers, magazines, the radio and electric signs were proclaiming to the world that a sensational new star had appeared in the movie heavens, that he was a dog and that his name was Strongheart. At every stop the train made crowds of people were on hand to acclaim the new celebrity, and in those cities where he was to make a theater appearance, special citizens formally welcomed him, hung a "key to the city" around his neck, and paraded him to the most important hotel where the best suite of rooms would be ready for him and his staff.

This wave of popularity was the result of a motion picture, written by Jane Murfin and directed by Larry Trimble, entitled *The Silent Call,* with Strongheart in the leading role and a cast of well-known Hollywood actors supporting him in the minor parts. The novelty of the production, the emotional and dramatic sweep of the story, the rugged outdoor backgrounds and the ir-resistible appeal of the big dog made the film a record-breaking success.

The success of *The Silent Call* sent Hollywood pro-ducers into a mad scramble to make dog pictures. Other German shepherd dogs were brought from Germany, new "sensational dog finds" were made in this country, and all hurried to Hollywood as starring material. But the incomparable Strongheart towered above them all in looks, character, accomplishments and audience appeal.

Following *The Silent Call* came other pictures, *Brawn of the North, The Love Master* and Jack London's *White Fang,* in all of which Strongheart played the leading roles, roles tailored to his exact measurements by Jane Murfin, roles which enabled him to demonstrate as never before how wonderfully intelligent and capable a dog can be when it is understood and given the right kind of co-operation. Each time a new film was released, thou-sands of enthusiasts were added to Strongheart's army of admirers.

With his fame reaching into every part of the world where motion pictures were shown, Strongheart became the Number One attraction in the world of entertainment, the most glittering of all the Hollywood stars, the monarch of all he surveyed. But at heart he was always "just a dog," with no greater ambition than simply to be of service and to share his all.

2. GOOD MAN FRIDAY

AT the height of all this glory there was an interruption in the busy Strongheart film-making schedule while new production plans were worked out. It was necessary for Larry Trimble and his assistants temporarily to leave California, and Strongheart went to live with Jane Murfin. Jane, however, received a hurry call to come to New York to help get one of her plays ready for a Broadway production. This created a major problem: what to do with their valuable four-legged property while she and Mr. Trimble were away from the city.

What Strongheart needed was a kind of Good Man Friday, someone to be with him continuously as a combination companion, valet, cook, chauffeur, secretary and private audience. This honor was conferred on me. Considering the fact that I knew practically nothing at all about dogs and had had almost no experience with them, the assignment was as surprising to me as I know it must have been to Strongheart. But Jane Murfin and Larry Trimble were old and understanding friends; there was a state of emergency; I had plenty of time available and a keen inclination for such an adventure.

Coming face to face with the real Strongheart for the

first time was like nothing I had ever experienced before. I had watched him in all of his pictures with the professional eye of a writer and a film producer. But I had not realized until this first meeting of ours how majestic, commanding and even awesome he was. I would no more have presumed to reach over and pat him on the head than I would have dared to pat the head of the President of the United States.

The man who brought Strongheart to our meeting place talked to the dog as though he were not an animal but an intelligent human being. Strongheart was told about the emergency situation, who I was, what I did for a living, and why I was there. He was told that until further notice he and I were to live together and do the best we could for each other.

Strongheart listened with alert attention, giving the impression that he understood everything that was said to him. Now and then he would turn his head in my direction and sweep me from head to feet with his eyes, as though deciding for himself whether the reports about me balanced with his own private appraisal. Then I was handed a list of instructions, the loop of a well-worn leash was placed around Strongheart's neck and the other end in my hand and that concluded the ceremony.

Strongheart and I headed for the little house in the Hollywood hills that I called home. As we walked along I began reading my instructions. I was told what and when to feed my new companion, how to bathe and brush him and what kind of exercise he should have every day. I was advised to treat him exactly as I would an intelligent human being. I was never under any circumstances to "talk down my nose" at him, to use baby talk with him, or to say anything to him with my lips that I did not sincerely mean in my heart. The instructions ended with the apparently serious recommendation that I read something worth while to him every day.

When we reached the house I turned the key in the front door, but before I could make the next move Strongheart pushed me aside, clamped his strong jaws on the knob, turned it, opened the door and marched in as though he owned the place. I meekly followed him in, wondering what it would please His Four-legged Highness to do next. It pleased him to give the entire house a going-over, like a seasoned police inspector who wanted to be sure just what went on under that particular roof. He carefully examined every room, every window, every entrance and every piece of furniture. He opened closet doors, stuck at least half of himself inside for looking and sniffing purposes, and then backed out again, closing the door behind him.

For some time I stood just inside the front door. Not once did he pay the slightest attention to me, and I had not the slightest idea what I should or should not do in the situation. I had supposed that a dog with his particular background, training and experience would wait for me, "his superior," to tell him what to do and when to do it. I had no idea that he would take over and manage things to suit himself. How were he and I ever going to get along together on the basis he seemed to be inaugurating?

Strongheart finally finished his inspection of the house. Then he marched with his military stride to where I was standing, gave the back of one of my hands a brief dab with his tongue and continued on out of doors to inspect the grounds surrounding the house. I interpreted the tongue dab to mean that he had found the house and its furnishings satisfactory, at least for the time being. But I did not know how he regarded me in this new arrangement of ours, or how I was to proceed in "taking care" of him. But while I did not know the answers, I intuitively felt that he probably did and that he might somehow or other be able to get the information across to me.

For the first time I understood how dumb a human can be in the presence of an intelligent animal.

3. GETTING ACQUAINTED

WHEN bedtime arrived, there came with it the question of where Strongheart was to sleep. His daylight activities had been carefully covered in the instructions, but no one had told me where he was accustomed to sleeping. He was too important a figure in the world of entertainment and motion pictures, it seemed to me, to be asked to sleep on the floor like an ordinary dog with perhaps an old blanket under him. But it was either the floor or into bed with me. Finally, after much consideration, I decided to share the bed with him.

After getting into my pajamas, I crawled to the far side of the bed, leaving the rest of it for Strongheart, the rest of it commanding the best views and being the official getting-in-and-out side. Strongheart had been keenly watching every move I made. Evidently he had been expecting just such an arrangement, for he immediately leaped onto the bed, towering above me in the dim lighting of the room in what seemed almost horse proportions. For some seconds he stared down at me and then began going round and round in a small circle, as though treading down invisible grass into suitable bedding for himself.

When the imaginary grass or whatever it was supposed to be had been arranged to his satisfaction, he flung himself down. But something was wrong for he got up again and began doing more of that circling and stamping, this time in the opposite direction. Finally satisfied, he dropped down again, let out a loud sigh and became very still. Taking this to mean that he was permanently down for the night, I switched out the light and let out a loud sigh too. The day's adventure was over, or so I thought.

On toward midnight, when our neighborhood was as quiet as all respectable neighborhoods should be at that hour, there was a number of sharp noises down the street, like an automobile engine backfiring; but Strongheart evidently interpreted it as gunfire, and he had been trained to do certain specific things when trouble like that started. So he took off. All 125 pounds of him! As he went out from his side of the bed he catapulted me out from my side onto the floor.

I got back into bed again, and several minutes later Strongheart returned from the adjoining room, having determined that it was a false alarm. Jumping up on the bed again, he made a few more circles and then flung himself down with his rear end up where his head should have been and his head toward the foot of the bed. I asked him to turn himself around. He did so, but most reluctantly.

About an hour later there was another noise outside. Again Strongheart went into action, and again I landed on the floor. As partial protection, not knowing what else to do, I pushed my side of the bed against the wall.

23

When Strongheart returned from his second false alarm he again lay down with his head toward the foot of the bed. Once again I had to ask him to turn himself around, and once again he did so, but as though he did not want to at all.

About dawn there was yet another noise outside the house and once again Strongheart bounded out of bed to see what was happening. This time I did not land on the floor; he merely flattened me against the wall. I was fed up with the whole adventure, particularly so when for the third time the dog lay down with his head toward the foot of the bed. He may have been loved by millions of people, but at that moment he was a collossal pain in the neck to me. I was sorry that I had ever met him socially.

With some bluster, I ordered him out of bed. He leaped to the floor, swung around and stood at military attention. I sat on the edge of the bed glaring at him.

"Listen, Strongheart," I said, "I am tired of having you kick me out of bed. It's got to stop. Do you understand? Furthermore, this sleeping upside down in bed, as you have been trying to do against my wishes and orders, has got to stop, too."

Strongheart stood with calm dignity, watching my face with unblinking eyes, an enigmatic expression on his face.

I continued: "You and I have to go on living with each other, whether we like the idea or not. Frankly, I don't like my part in it at all, but we're stuck with each other. I am willing to make allowances for the way you have been jumping out of bed when you hear suspicious

24

noises, since you are a police dog. But this sleeping with your rear end where your head ought to be is *out!*"

At this point Strongheart suddenly moved forward, closed his jaws on one of my pajama sleeves and tugged me gently but firmly to the foot of the bed. A short distance away were some rather insecure old French windows covered by long curtains. Getting an end of one of these in his teeth Strongheart pulled it back, held it there for a few seconds and then let it drop back into position again. Then he began barking, swinging his head rhythmically back and forth between the French windows and me.

Had he spoken in perfect English he could not have told me more clearly what he wanted me to know: that whenever he lay down to relax either temporarily or for his night sleep, he always wanted to have the front end of himself—his eyes, nose, ears and jaws—aimed in the direction of possible danger. If trouble did enter in human form, he could go into action without having to lose time by turning around. And those old French windows were certainly a possible trouble entrance.

Strongheart had been leaping out of bed to investigate suspicious noises, and he had been lying upsidedown in bed, not to please himself but to take care of me as he had been taught to do. As this became clear to be, I experienced a kind of humility I had never known before. We compromised the situation by turning the bed around so that we could both lie with our heads in the direction of the suspicious old French windows.

4. PUZZLEMENT

STRONGHEART was so pleased with the new arrangement that he gave the side of my face a couple of dabs with his tongue, heaved a deep sigh, relaxed like an old shirt that had been dropped into a laundry basket and went serenely to sleep.

But there was no sleep for me. I was wide awake with amazement. I had spoken to Strongheart in my kind of language, a language of thoughts and feelings incased in human sound symbols. He had actually been able to receive and understand what I had said. Then he had answered me in his kind of language, a language made up of simple sounds and pantomime which he obviously felt I could follow without too much difficulty. Strongheart had understood me perfectly, and then with his keen and penetrating dog wisdom he had made it possible for me to understand him, too.

For the first time, I was actually conscious of being in rational correspondence with an animal. With the dog's patient and guiding help, we had been able to communicate our individual states of mind to each other, to exchange points of view and thereby to solve a difficulty that threatened to mar our relationship. His innate wis-

26

dom had topped my intellectual reasoning at every point. I realized how little I knew about the mental capacities of a dog and his ability to express those capacities in a practical way.

I had been privileged to watch an animal, acting upon its own initiative, put into expression qualities of independent thinking . . . of clear reasoning . . . of good judgment . . . of foresight . . . of prudence . . . of common sense. I had been taught to believe that these qualities belonged more or less exclusively to the members of the human species, or rather to the "educated members" of our species. And here was a dog overflowing with them!

Hour after hour I lay there listening to Strongheart's deep, regular breathing, trying to unriddle him. But the more I worked at it the more puzzling he became. At dawn, while he slumbered peacefully on, I was still surrounded by spinning question marks, still reviewing all sorts of beliefs having to do with animals in general and dogs in particular. One thing was clear: I certainly was taking care of something far greater and more significant than "just a dog" as I had been accustomed to evaluating a dog. And I saw that the important thing for me to know about Strongheart was not so much his physical body but rather his larger invisible embodiment of thoughts, feelings and character.

It occurred to me that if I were ever going to be able to keep really rational company with this amazing dog by my side, I would have to begin doing two important things at once: first, find out all that I could about Strongheart as a mental entity; and second, try in all possible ways to discover how we were related as individual expressions of life in a highly intelligent universe.

It became apparent that "something" which could well be spelled with a capital "S" had already linked Strongheart and me in inseparable kinship, even though he walked the earth on four legs and I only on two, and even though, according to popular human belief, that dog and I appeared to be so unrelated in so many different ways.

But how, I wondered, does one go about solving such kinship mysteries between himself and a dog? Who, or what, does he consult for the right directions? Or is it wiser to do such exploring alone, following one's own inner leadings?

5. KEEPING COMPANY

IT was not easy to qualify as a companion for the
famous dog movie star. The difficulty was Strongheart
himself. He was too mysterious, too self-contained, too
capable, too much a "sacred cow" for one with my
limited knowledge of dogs. What I really rated was a
more common specimen, a dog, say, from the city animal
shelter who not only needed a friend but had to have one
in order to escape the fate of unwanted animals.

Strongheart was the most extraordinary animal I had
ever come upon in any part of the world. He was particularly distinctive in his thinking processes, in the way
he could reason things through for himself, arrive at his
own conclusions and then translate those conclusions into
practical action without human assistance. Such inde-
pendence and wisdom in a dog was hard to believe even
while watching it in operation.

Strongheart had many toys sent to him by admirers
from all parts of the world, and he was very fond of
playing with them. When he was in the mood for this
kind of fun he would open the closet door where the
toys were kept, study them for a while, then pick up the
one he fancied with his teeth, back out, carefully close

the door behind him, and take the toy out into the yard and play with it. When he had had enough of this kind of fun, he would bring his toy back into the house again, open the closet door, place the plaything exactly where he had found it, and then back out, carefully closing the door behind him.

If he saw me begin any work—bed making, house cleaning, moving furniture, washing the car or working in the garden—he would always insist upon helping, using his jaws in place of hands, and always making a real contribution.

I had been authorized to take full charge of Strong-heart and to manage all of his private and public activities, but he began reversing this arrangement minutes after we had been left together; he took charge of me as though he were the human and I the dog. His background, of course, had included police and war work, so he was accustomed to taking charge of people and things. He was not the kind of a dog one would care to dispute matters of this kind with, not with his physical setup and combat record. He accepted me readily enough as his emergency associate, as he had been told to do, but he usually gave the impression that he was really in charge and that any authority I assumed was a temporary concession.

I had always considered it my privilege and right to go to bed at whatever time it pleased me to do so, and to get up again whenever I felt like it, providing, of course, that I was not acting contrary to duty. But Strong-heart did not approve of this habit, probably because of his strict military training in Germany.

His custom was to bounce out of bed at precisely six o'clock every morning, full of energy, spontaneity and enthusiasm. He did not have to be let out; he would open all the doors and let himself out. There was an old door between the bedroom and living room which now and then would resist him on his way out. This he regarded as personal effontery. He would make danger sounds in his throat, clamp his powerful jaws on the knob and, throwing all of his 125 pounds into the effort, pull the old door off its hinges.

Within the hour he would come racing back into the bedroom again, supercharged with fresh air, vitality and excitement, and start flinging barks at me to advise me that it was time for me to be up, around and doing, especially in connection with his breakfast. If there was no response he would pull all the clothes off the bed and drag them to the far side of the room. If that did not get results, he would take hold of my pajamas and tug on them until either I or a section of the pajamas left with him. In the evening when he had decided that I had been up long enough, he would begin barking and pulling at my clothes to inform me officially that it was time for me to quit whatever I was doing and retire for the night. If I happened to have a book in my hands he would often snatch it from me, run into the adjoining room with it and drop it on the bed to let me know that that was where I belonged until further orders from him.

Like nearly all dogs, as well as practically all children that have not been blocked in their natural growing and expanding, Strongheart was a master of the art of living fully and completely in the here and now of things. He

31

always made the immediate occasion and the immediate circumstance yield some kind of a dividend in interest and fun. Even when he seemed to be sleeping this magic still went on; for his body would vibrate, twitch, jerk and jump as he participated in all kinds of adventure in the kingdom of his own imagination.

Strongheart clearly believed that life is for living and sharing as fully as possible and that the world is not an arena but a playground. He began showing me how our relationship could be turned into a continuous holiday. Parts of this holiday we observed at home and the rest exploring open country. The holidays at home resulted from duties which could not be avoided; while I attended to these Strongheart would entertain himself. He sensed that I was not to be disturbed when I was at work at my desk, and he never intentionally did so. He was a constant interrupter nevertheless, because I could not resist watching him and the interesting things he did under his own planning and initiative.

Durng these at-home occasions, Strongheart would put on his own private shows. He was the producer and manager, the entertainer, the entertainment and the audience, too. He was the whole show, and he never gave himself a dull moment. If dullness did creep in, he would quit and do something else. The only other living things he ever shared these playtimes with were bugs. They fascinated and delighted him. Whenever he found one crawling along the ground, he would trail it with intense curiosity and friendliness, trying to find out where the little fellow was going and what it would do when it got there.

Perhaps the most unforgettable of those shows of his were the ones he put on with an old shoe that he had found on one of our walks and for which he had a great fondness. He executed four-legged dance patterns with the old shoe as a kind of symbol which he alone knew how to interpret; he did dramatic play vignettes in which the old shoe seemed to serve as an emblem for everything he liked or did not like. And he gave just as magnificent a performance playing with that old shoe in the back yard with no one but me watching him as he did in front of motion-picture cameras or admiring and applauding theater audiences.

6. MIND READER

AS day followed day in our retreat in the Hollywood hills, far removed from the parade grounds of the current movie gods and goddesses, the stalking publicity hounds and the ceaseless noises of the publicity sirens, the more wonderful and incomprehensible Strongheart became to me. The part of him with which I slept, ate, walked and played was relatively easy to understand. But not the mental part of him. Not the mysterious, invisible portion of him that functioned so effectively back of his physical exterior and enabled him to do the extraordinary things he did.

Then one day something happened which gave to our relationship entirely new meaning and direction. It was a particularly beautiful spring morning after many days of rain. From the Pacific Ocean shifting wind brought an exhilarating salt tang, and from the desert country in the opposite direction a warm scent of sage. It was not the kind of day for anyone to be sitting at a desk fingering a typewriter; nor was it the kind of weather to be experienced merely through open doors and windows.

"Shall I be a man and finish this writing job?" I asked myself. "Or shall I be a mouse, quit the whole thing and take Strongheart into the hills for the rest of the day and evening?"

There was not much argument; I decided to be a mouse.

Within a few seconds after this decision had been made, the back door was knocked violently open and in rushed Strongheart in a frenzy of excitement. Skidding to where I was sitting he gave the back of one of my hands a brief dab with his tongue, raced into the bedroom and came out almost immediately with the old sweater I always wore on our outings. Then into the bedroom again and back with my bluejeans. Then came one of my walking boots. Then its mate. Then my Irish walking stick. All of these things he carefully placed at my feet. In five swiftly executed trips into the bedroom, he had brought to me all the things I needed for our trip into the back country. Then bouncing, and swirling, and barking with everything he could put into it, he made it clear that he felt we should leave at once, and sooner if possible.

I stared at him in stunned amazement. How did the dog know that I had changed my plans and was going to take him on an outing? There had been no outward communication between us at all. As a matter of fact, I had not known where he was except in a general way for some hours. In the supposed privacy of my own mind I had suddenly changed intention, and then he appeared on the scene knowing all about it.

Until late into the night Strongheart and I wandered about in the hill country, he looking for adventure while I trailed after him, as intellectually dizzy and confused as I have ever been in my life. As we were nearing home on the return trip, it came to me that Strongheart had been reading my mind in this manner ever since our first meeting but that I had not been alert or wise enough to notice it before. I began to recall time after time when Strongheart must have known my intentions and plans before I had been able to set them in outward motion.

"How does he do it?" I kept asking myself over and over again as I followed him down the trail. "Is this mind-reading ability something that is innate and natural in all dogs, perhaps in all animals, or is it a kind of special endowment that only a dog like Strongheart would have, and that someone may have helped him bring into expression?"

I thought and thought, but there were no satisfying answers, nothing but the unavoidable proof that this dog could tap my mind and read my inmost thoughts with ease and accuracy whenever he cared to do so.

I began to read innumerable books about dogs. These provided a lot of material about selecting, breeding, caring for, training, exhibiting and selling a dog to the best advantage, but none of them took me any nearer to understanding how Strongheart was able to read my private thinking. Here and there an author would begin to move in this general direction, only to veer off again and begin writing about dogs merely as biological specimens with certain professionally agreed upon price-tag values.

These books all dealt in physical effects rather than in the mental causes back of the effects. What I needed was someone to explain to me the mental part of a dog; to tell me about that invisible and mysterious "whatever-it-is" that makes dogs what they so delightfully are. None of the writers I read seemed to regard such an approach as important.

Then I began consulting in person all kinds of amateur and professional dog experts, from dog catchers to internationally known dog-show judges. Practically all of them had had many experiences in which dogs had read their thinking as easily and as accurately as Strongheart had mine. All of them had known dogs that had been able mentally to foresee and foretell events before they happened in outward experience. But not one had been sufficiently interested to investigate such challenging phenomena.

Whenever I would ask one of these experts to explain to me what it was that enabled a dog to read human thinking, as all dogs appeared to be capable of doing, and actually to see or otherwise sense invisible things, he would talk at considerable length and end by telling me that it was a "natural instinct" that nearly all dogs have in some degree.

I would ask him what he meant by the term "a natural instinct," and how it functioned not only with a dog but between a dog and a human; then he would resume the flow of words and technical terms and disappear in a professional fog, leaving me right where I was when I started.

7. *MASTER DETECTIVE*

ONE day a distinguished-looking, soft-spoken foreigner with great charm of manner came to visit Strongheart and me. He introduced himself as an author who had been specially sent to California by a famous European publisher to do a series of magazine articles about Strongheart which were later to appear in book form. For some time he plied me with intimate questions about the big dog as though he were a prosecuting attorney. He asked how Strongheart had been prepared for motion pictures, how he was handled in front of the cameras, and how certain results were obtained in certain films.

When he found out that I had had nothing at all to do with the dog's films or the dog's training but was merely taking care of him while his owner, producers and director were out of town, the man's interest in me dropped to the zero point and he became rather surly. I could not quite understand this sudden change in manner. To relieve the situation I suggested that he accompany me outdoors where I would be happy to introduce him to Strongheart and then he could observe and write whatever he pleased.

Strongheart was walking leisurely across the back lawn

as we came out. Seeing us he stopped abruptly with one of his front paws off the ground and began staring at our visitor with a look in his eyes that I had never seen there before. The hair around his neck went straight up. Then he charged. The man by my side turned and started running toward the back door, but he was too late. Strongheart caught him by one of his ankles, threw him flat, seized one of his arms, and flopped him over on his back. The dog's fangs swept back and forth just off the man's chin as though he were about to rip out his throat. It was almost as terrifying for me as it was for the man. Fortunately for him he remained motionless.

I managed to get Strongheart away and to get the man back into the house. He was frightened and considerably shaken up, and he left threatening us with all kinds of legal action as well as plenty of bad publicity.

I was greatly annoyed at Strongheart for the mess he had gotten us into and wondered what I ought to do about the trouble that was headed our way. But he was just as calm and philosophical about it as though nothing inharmonious had taken place at all. I wondered if it were possible that Strongheart had detected something in the visitor's motives that warranted that kind of treatment.

Before sundown the following day, I had a complete "undercover" record of our visitor. He was not a writer at all; he was not connected with any publisher; nor was he any of the other things that he had pretended to be. He was a professional dog trainer and he had brought a German shepherd dog to Hollywood in the hope of getting it into motion pictures and making a fortune for himself. A rather vague, tentative contract awaited him, I learned, provided that he could find out the secret of how Strongheart did the remarkable things he did in front of the cameras and could then top him with his own dog. The man had bluffed me completely with his appearance and pretense, but not for a second did he fool Strongheart.

On another occasion Strongheart and I happened to be in a large office building in Los Angeles and stopped in to say hello to a lawyer friend. He was so delighted at meeting the famous dog for the first time that he wanted his legal partner, who was in a conference in an adjoining office, to meet him, too. As we entered his partner was sitting at a large desk with two men at either end of it. All three got to their feet at once and began staring at Strongheart like fascinated children. Suddenly and without the slightest warning Strongheart began barking threateningly and lunged at the man standing at the right of the desk. He did not quite reach him; the chokestrap around his neck prevented it; but for the next few minutes the room was filled with excitement as the other four men made exits as fast as they could. They had really seen Strongheart in action. I finally got the dog out of the room, but it took everything I had to accomplish it.

When things were quieted down I apologized to my lawyer friend for the disturbance that we had caused. I also told him what I had been discovering about the dog's ability to read the thoughts and motives of those about him. The lawyer, being a dog owner himself and also something of a philosopher, was deeply interested.

40

By way of testing what I had told him I suggested that he find out all he could about the real motives and intentions of the man that Strongheart had tried to attack. This was done, and to the astonishment of both lawyers, the man was found to be one of the most dishonest big-deal promoters in the country. He was later indicted. He had a charming personality; he moved in the best social circles; and he had successfully bluffed and preyed upon innumerable wealthy people for years, but he could not fool the dog.

I did not have to be within range of Strongheart's physical observation for him correctly to read my thinking and know all about my plans. He could do it across distances as easily as though he were sitting at my side. For instance, once or twice each week I would have luncheon at a Los Angeles club that was over a dozen miles away from where Strongheart and I lived. Whenever I did this a friend would stay at the house and keep an eye on the dog. There was never any set time for my returning, but at the precise moment when I decided to leave the club and come home Strongheart would always quit whatever he happened to be doing, take himself to his favorite spot for observation, and patiently wait there for me to turn the bend in the road and head up the hill.

8. DAWDLING

PRACTICALLY everything that passed between Strongheart and me by way of communication, silent or otherwise, moved in only one direction: from me to him. He never seemed to have the least difficulty in sensing my unexpressed thoughts, feelings, intentions and plans, but I could never fathom what he was planning unless he barked it across to me or used a simple form of pantomime with his body.

Day after day and night after night I carefully studied almost everything that Strongheart did. I seldom gave him orders. He was allowed all possible freedom. He could really be himself and express himself just as he pleased.

Then without warning another one of "those things" happened. Strongheart and I were observing one of our most favored pastimes. We had barred the doors to all visitors, shut off the telephone, and given ourselves over to the almost totally lost art of dawdling, of lazy, lingering loafing, of doing nothing at all with determination. Strongheart was highly proficient in this art. Whenever he had anything to do he flung everything he had into it, but when there was nothing of special interest to engage his attention he would loosen everything and just dawdle.

Strongheart and I were lying on the floor of the living room dawdling. He was stretched out and I was flat on my back with my head on his ribs. The weightiest matter I had on my mind was the drowsy wish that everyone could feel as comfortable and as satisfied with life as I did at that moment. Every little while Strongheart would sound off with a deep sigh of contentment and thump his tail on the floor to let me know that all was well with him, too.

In the midst of this dawdling something seemed to explode in the middle of my mind, blasting all the loafing out of me and setting me straight up on the floor. Strongheart must have felt a similar inner impact too, for he scrambled to his feet, looked quizzically about in all directions, then sat down and began staring at me with an intent expression on his face. He just stared, and stared, and stared. All that I could think of to do was to stare back at him.

My guess was that something of a mental nature having to do with our relationship had just taken place, and that Strongheart was trying in his wordless manner to get it across to me. I tried to become as inwardly attentive and as receptive as possible. For a while nothing seemed to happen. Then I began to get a not particularly distinct mental impression to this effect: that if I really wanted to get at the facts about this big dog I would have to stop localizing him within the boundaries of his body and begin to look for him in more expansive categories.

43

Strongheart got to his feet, shook himself vigorously, walked the length of the room and back and then stretched himself out on the floor, making it crystal clear that his part in the proceedings was at an end. He was returning to his dawdling and the thumping of his tail on the floor indicated that he felt I should do the same thing.

But I was through with dawdling. I had immediate and serious work to do. I felt that I *must* unriddle the increasingly bewildering twists and turns that our adventure was taking.

Each of us, I knew, was an individual expression of life and intelligence. And that being plainly so, I assured myself, then somewhere there *had* to be a point of contact where he and I could meet with perfect understanding. But how, I wondered, does one go about accomplishing such a feat in human-dog relationships? How find out about that unseen individuality of his, operating behind his physical individuality? To whom could I turn for help?

Suddenly it occurred to me that I had completely forgotten to get in touch with the one man who really could help me to solve the enigma of Strongheart. But could I find this man? And having found him, could I persuade him to help me? At dawn the next morning I was headed for the Mojave Desert.

9. DESERT RAT

HE is known as a desert rat. The only name he has had for many years is Mojave Dan, but that is all he ever needs. He loves the desert, and it is constantly revealing to him its deepest secrets. His "family" consists of an assortment of dogs and burros; often wild animals become temporary members. Dan has practically no social or economic standing but he is rich in the kind of things that can never be taken away from him, now or in eternity.

He is one of the freest men I have ever known. He has no obligations, no responsibilities, no cares, no fears and no worries. When he needs supplies for his "family" and himself, he knows where to go to pan enough gold to pay for them. He never takes from the earth more gold than is necessary for his modest requirements. He goes where he pleases when he pleases, and he does what he pleases in the way that it pleases him to do it.

Because of his unpredictable wandering habits it is often difficult to locate Dan. The desert where he lives has an enormous spread, and he may be in any part of it. I very much wanted to get in touch with him because up to that time he was the only human I had ever personally known who could carry on silent two-way conversations with animals and really share ideas with them. Dan never reads books, magazines or newspapers, never listens to the radio, never watches television and seldom asks questions of other humans; yet he is amazingly well-informed at all times about practically everything that interests him, either near by or afar. This information comes from his dogs and burros, from wild animals, from snakes, from insects, from birds, indeed from almost everything that crosses his trail. The real mystery was not so much Dan's ability silently to communicate his thoughts to the animal but his capacity to understand when the animal spoke to him.

I had upon a number of occasions tried to get Dan to tell me how he went about establishing such practical correspondence with nonhuman forms of life, but he would never do so. None of his other friends could get the secret out of him either. His reply to these requests was that such things were too intimate to talk about and could be acquired only through personal effort and real humility.

I did not take Strongheart with me on the trip, much as I wanted him and Dan to know each other. The desert at that time of the year was much too hot for the big dog; very reluctantly I left him behind, which he did not approve of at all.

Arriving at a little desert town where Dan occasionally went to buy supplies, I found I was in luck. He had been there earlier in the day, and I was able to make a good guess at the spot in the desert he planned to spend the night. A few hours later Dan and I were having supper together, companioned by his dogs and burros, his old tent, a camp fire and the desert. After the dishes had been washed and stowed away, Dan and I lay on our backs and communed with the stars; in that clear atmosphere they seemed very near. There had been little conversation between Dan and me during the preparation of the meal or while eating; Dan goes in for such things, even with his friends, as little as possible. He believes that needless talk not only wastes energy but pollutes the atmosphere. He is a strict observer of the ancient desert rule that if you cannot improve on the desert silence then you should keep your mouth shut.

But I thought there was some excuse for a certain amount of talking on this occasion; I had a major problem in human-animal relationships and had come a long distance to ask Dan's advice. I told him how Strongheart and I happened to be living together; I told him of the difficulty I was having in getting at the real truth about the big dog; and I asked him what he thought I should do next.

There was no response at all from Dan. Just the desert silence. A silence so intense that it was rather disturbing to my city-sound-accustomed ears. Patiently I waited . . . and waited . . . and waited. But not a sound or a movement did my friend make. One of two things seemed to have happened: either what I had said did not interest him, or he had gone to sleep.

Much more time elapsed. Finally Dan yawned and stretched. Then he spoke, aiming his words at the stars. "There's facts about dogs," he said, "and there's opinions about them. The dogs have the facts, and the humans

47

have the opinions. If you want facts about a dog, always get them straight from the dog. If you want opinions, get them from the human."

A real expert on human-animal relationships had spoken. Having done so, he rolled over on his side and this time definitely went to sleep. In those few words, Dan had given me just the help I needed. He had shown me clearly where I had been making my basic mistake in the Strongheart situation. I had consulted almost every kind of an authority I could find about Strongheart, except Strongheart himself! As the sun arose over the distant desert horizon line the following morning, I headed back for Hollywood and Strongheart.

10. DOG INTERVIEW

I NOW set about following Mojave Dan's advice. I intended to get the facts about Strongheart straight from the dog himself, rather than depending upon human opinions. Strongheart, I knew, would have little difficulty in following most of the things I said. But how was I going to be able to understand him?

For our first experiment I got Strongheart to sit on the living-room floor with me, so that we could look into each other's eyes and, I hoped, into each other's minds and hearts. Then I began talking to him as though he were another and very intelligent human being. I told him about the trip to the desert, why I had gone there and what Dan had said about by-passing humans with their opinions and going straight to a dog for the facts about that dog.

"And that's the reason we are sitting here on the floor," I added. "I am interviewing you about yourself, and about us. There are a lot of things about you that baffle me, things that have to be solved so that I can keep better company with you. I've read all kinds of books and consulted all sorts of so-called authorities, but none of them was able to get me any nearer to understanding you. Then over in the desert I learned that you yourself are the proper authority to consult. You have all the facts about yourself. I shall appreciate it if you will share some of these facts with me, for the greater good of both of us. I don't know how you are going to be able to do it; that will have to be up to you."

Strongheart sat there as though posing for a still picture for one of his films. He was keenly alert, with his head cocked a trifle off center, his ears straight up and funneled in my direction, and his eyes following every movement of my lips.

I asked him question after question. I asked about human-animal relationships in general; I asked many questions about himself, in particular. I asked each question very slowly, then paused, often for several minutes, for some kind of a response, but there was none. He did nothing at all, as far as I was able to observe, except just to sit there as though made of stone and stare at me with an expression on his face that could have been interpreted as almost anything.

At last I ran out of questions. I waited and waited, but not one observable contribution did Strongheart make to the occasion. Occasionally he blinked his eyes and wiggled the end of his nose. The silence was profound. I made up my mind that I would outsit and outstare the dog if it took the rest of the night. Finally Strongheart yawned, got to his feet, shook himself, turned around, marched to the end of the room with his precise military stride, opened the door and disappeared into the night. The interview was at an end.

It was discouraging, but there was a faint ray of hope. Just as Strongheart's tail went out the back door, I had a sudden intuitive inkling as to why the interview had been a failure. Strongheart, this inkling intimated quite as though someone had whispered to me, had been trying to communicate with me as we sat there on the floor, but I had lacked the ability to understand what he was silently saying. So he had finally had to adjourn the meeting until I was better prepared for being in rational correspondence with a dog.

The effort to establish a medium of practical intercommunication between the dog and myself became a major quest. I followed every line of procedure that suggested itself, no matter how fantastic. Most of the way it was bewildering and challenging, like seeking a desired objective through dense, swirling fog. I failed to understand how the dog could make such accurate contact with my thinking processes, while I could not tap his thinking at all, except in the most crude and obvious kind of way.

Through as much of every twenty-four hours as possible, I continued to keep Strongheart under the closest surveillance, watching every move he made and trying to find the exact mental reason for it. Every day as part of my Good Man Friday duties, I read to him. Of course, I could not understand why a dog, even a dog as distinguished as Strongheart, should be read to or what good could possibly come of it. I even suspected that it might be some kind of a comedy gag. But I included it in our daily program nevertheless, partly because I had been told to do so, partly out of curiosity to see what would come of it and partly because it added such a whimsical oddity to the adventure itself.

51

Every morning Strongheart and I would sit facing each other, either on our living-room floor or somewhere out of doors, and I would share the contents of books, magazines and newspapers with him, taking care that he got the best in subject matter as well as in literary expression. He always listened with polite attention, as though understanding and enjoying everything that was said. But whenever he took the focus of his eyes off my lips and yawned, that was always the sign that he was bored; it was automatically the end of the reading session.

One morning after I had finished reading some unusually fine poetry to him and we were looking off into the distances from our high, grassy point of vantage, it suddenly occurred to me why I had been instructed to read something worth while to Strongheart every day. The more I had read to Strongheart the more I had been mentally lifting him out of all kinds of limiting dog classifications and balancing life with him as an intelligent fellow being, a fellow being who was entitled to as much of the best of everything as I hoped to enjoy myself. As our shared days rolled adventurously and educationally along, I made another interesting and illuminating discovery: the more I stopped treating Strongheart like "a dog" in the conventional meaning of the term, the more he stopped acting like "a dog," at least as far as I was concerned. And the more this fascinating thing happened, the more we began functioning as rational companions and the more the kinship barriers between us came tumbling down.

11. CURRICULUM

ONE day I ran into a kind of impasse with Strongheart in which he again became a complete enigma to
me. Something was definitely blocking the way. Much to
my private embarrassment, I finally found out what it
was: ME! With all my well-intentioned efforts, I had
been making the common ego mistake of trying to do all
the thinking and to arrive at all the final conclusions for
both of us. It just would not work that way, even with a
dog.

The only solution was to do a complete all-out in following the valuable advice Mojave Dan had given me. I
had been doing so only partly. There had been altogether
too much of ME as a self-appointed knower, and not
enough of Strongheart and what he might have to share
as an intelligent expression of life. Without being aware
of the unfair thing I had been doing, I had mentally
assigned myself to the upper part of this relationship of
ours, because I happened to be "a human," and had
mentally assigned him to the lower part, because he was
"a dog."

I decided to do a complete right-about-face. I would
heave all human-animal traditions and conventions over-

board, reverse the customary procedure of "man trains dog," and instead make it "dog trains man." I would try to set aside all pride in self and species, to quit all intellectual resistance, to become as humble and as receptive as I know how, to let the dog really go to work on me in an educational way. That would certainly be fulfilling Mojave Dan's advice about going directly to a dog to get the facts about that dog.

Strongheart became "the professor," I was the "entire student body," and wherever we happened to be, either indoors or out, became our "classroom." That is how the curriculum functioned as long as Strongheart's physical body was bouncing around in the earth scene. And that is how it still functions. He is still my teacher, and I am still his pupil. Through the illusory mists of time and even death itself, he continues to share with me, through the eternality of goodness, things that are exceedingly important for me to know and to practice.

It was such an irregular curriculum and so far outside all academic sanctions that until the results justified a sharing of the facts, it had to be kept a profound secret. I knew what rigidly set, bristling opinions most humans cherish in all matters having to do with education, when it comes to defining what qualifies one living being "to impart knowledge, skill and the discipline of character to another living being." I could imagine what would happen if an animal were seriously recommended as a well-equipped teacher for humans.

The only equipment that Professor Strongheart and I used in our educational system was a book of synonyms, a dictionary, and a notebook and pencil. These, of course, were for me. My teacher-and-trainer needed only himself, a bit of encouragement from me, my undivided attention, and enough space in which to operate. My study period was practically continuous; as long as Strongheart was observable, school was in session and I was being taught.

Our curriculum was flexible, unpredictable, practical—and full of fun. It was by no means an easy course. I had a large assortment of wrong beliefs about dogs and other animals; these notions had to be cleared out in order to make room for the facts. It took discipline . . . a sense of wonder and appreciation . . . inner and outer flexibility . . . unlimited expectancy . . . and a willingness to follow facts wherever they led.

All that Strongheart had to do as instructor was to be himself. My part was carefully to watch everything he did and search for character qualities in him. My book of synonyms aided me to find the names of qualities, and the dictionary gave me a more thorough meaning of the qualities. Then I would list these qualities in my notebook and study just what he did with them in his moment-by-moment living.

I did not look merely for "good dog qualities," as they are usually listed by dog-show judges and other professionals. I was searching for the universal best in qualities, regardless of species identification. For qualities of abiding worth. For the kind of qualities that we humans always respect and honor whenever we find them in the members of our own species. Even for the kind of qualities that all the great world teachers agree are essential for living the superior life.

I found hundreds upon hundreds of these great qualities in Strongheart. They came welling up in all their purity and glory from deep within him. He diffused them as naturally and as irresistibly as a flower does its perfume, a bird its song, a child its laughter.

This curriculum of ours was, and still is, completely without academic sanction; nevertheless I recommend it to you, especially if your relationship contacts, whether with humans or animals, have become restricted, flat, meaningless and otherwise unprofitable. Should you decide to give it a trial, either with your own dog or some other kind of animal, you can be assured of richly rewarding results.

It is not necessary to have a dog as accomplished and as famous as Strongheart in order to make this unorthodox curriculum work successfully. A specially bred dog is not required. Nor is a trained one. Any old kind of a dog will do, as long as it wags its tail at your approach. Not even excluding some "dirty little mongrel" that you may have come upon while it was snatching a bit of much-needed dinner from an overturned garbage pail. Sooner or later the observant human comes to discover that practically every dog is innately equipped with valuable knowledge and wisdom and is a master in the art of teaching humans by means of the irresistible power of a silent good example.

12. LOOK AND SEE

DRIVING down the coast of Southern California on a particularly lovely summer morning, when everything everywhere was proclaiming the wisdom, friendliness and glory of the Creator of it all, Professor Strongheart and I at last found what we had been looking for: our kind of beach. It had plenty of hard sand and was deserted by everything except seabirds. We had to have it that way; my four-legged private instructor was too valuable an entertainment investment to risk having encounters with other dogs or with certain kinds of humans that he seemed to feel were not nice people to have around, even on a pleasant summer day.

Unpacking our lunch, a blanket, some books and a few other things, we established school headquarters on top of a sandhill from which there was an unrestricted view in all directions. Always sharing all that I possibly could with Strongheart, even the work on these trips, I let him help bring the various things from the car and assist in arranging them. This he did with great skill, considering his lack of hands. When everything was in place and I was sitting cross-legged in the middle of the blanket, I gave him the formal nod for which he had been impatiently waiting and off he raced as fast as his legs could carry him. At that moment school began for me.

With distance in his eyes, his energy full-on, hard sand under his feet, an ocean to dash into whenever he felt the urge and no one to boss him, Strongheart was a magnificent object to watch, much more so at such times, indeed, than in his films, great as these films were. In making motion pictures he always had to operate within certain restricted and carefully regulated patterns in order to blend his actions with those of the human actors and thus harmonize the flow of the story. But on a deserted beach, with no one to interfere with his mental and physical action, he provided superthrilling entertainment every second. Part of the time he performed on the beach, part of the time in the ocean, and the rest of the time he relaxed and planned what to do next.

I never tired of being student-audience for him during these beach sessions. His zest for living . . . his vitality . . . his powerful and almost catlike agility . . . his enthusiasm . . . his sense of wonder and appreciation . . . his complete interest in the immediate thing he was doing . . . all these were delightfully educational and entertaining. He had a tremendous ability to extract fun, happiness and satisfaction out of each moment, and he never permitted life to become uninteresting, either for himself or for those around him.

Watching him that day as his student-observer, with the Pacific Ocean giving him just the kind of a background he needed, I could not recall when I had seen more majestic composition, or more perfect co-ordination in action. It was as if a poem had assumed the form of a

58

dog in order to express in meaning and rhythm what could not possibly be said in written or spoken words. All that Strongheart was exhibiting in physical form and in action out there on the beach was simply the expression of his splendid character, the radiation in endless living combinations of his truly great inner qualities, the very qualities I had been finding in him day by day with the help of my book of synonyms and dictionary.

Then I knew that what I was actually being privileged to watch was not a dog expressing great qualities, but rather, great qualities expressing a dog. He was radiating them from deep within himself, flinging them out as freely and as lavishly as the sun does its rays. He was not trying in the least to achieve this effect; he was just letting it happen.

Finally somewhat weary with his strenuous rompings, Strongheart came to where I was sitting and flung himself down. He did not shut his eyes as he usually did when relaxing in this manner. Instead, he looked up into my face with unusual warmth and thumped his tail on the sand. He seemed to have something on his mind that he very much wanted me to know; he was doing his best to share it with me, but I could not get it, not even in a general sort of way.

Softly the scene slid into a brilliant starlit night filled with fragrance of the sea and land. Strongheart and I now sat shoulder to shoulder, looking off into the darkness with shared wonder and delight. I quit trying to discover what my four-legged companion had on his mind, and he and I relaxed and became just parts of the night, along with the seabirds, the stars, the ocean and the sand.

Then I had another of those revealing experiences that were becoming more and more frequent in my relationship adventure with Strongheart. Without the least conscious effort on my part, I would suddenly come into possession of important facts that I had never known before. This particular bit of unexpected knowledge was embarrassing. I suddenly knew that while I had come in contact with hundreds upon hundreds of dogs, all kinds and conditions of dogs in many different parts of the world, yet in all that experience and with all these opportunities for intelligent observation, I had never actually *seen* a dog! I had merely *looked* at dogs, without being able really to *see* one of them.

Slowly I began to realize what had been going on as I watched Strongheart playing on the beach earlier in the day . . . what had been silently taking place as he lay on the sand near me looking up into my face and thumping his tail . . . and what was still going on as we sat in the darkness. In his own simple way, Strongheart was working a mighty miracle on me. The miracle of opening my blind inner eyes—so that I could really *see* a dog when I looked at one.

13. EYEBALLS

THE embarrassing discovery that I had been unable actually to see a dog when I looked at one began breaking down all sorts of barriers between Strongheart and me. It gave fresh impetus, new direction, and greater purpose to our relationship.

When we first began living together, my attitude toward Strongheart had been the conventional one. I assigned myself a place high in the scale of values because I was "a human," and gave him a place far below because he happened to be "a dog." I did this regardless of his unusual accomplishments, his world-wide fame and the large sum of money that he could earn for others. I had long been under the impression that while I lived in the upper levels of existence, all animals, not even excluding Strongheart, had to do their living on much lower and relatively unimportant mental and physical levels; and that between them and myself there could be certain rather limited service ties, but not much else. These ideas were to be radically changed.

When I began my "dog-trains-man" experiment with Strongheart, I was compelled to learn that if I wanted to achieve complete awareness of him, or of any other living thing, I would have to use something far more penetrating and perceptive with which to see than just a couple of eyeballs in my skull peering out through upper and lower lids.

I had to discard my eyeballs as reliable reporting factors, so to speak, and to begin using my thinking to see with. This practice is not so fantastic as it may at first appear. It has long and distinguished precedence, established by some of the wisest men and women throughout all history. Practically all of them, it is interesting to note, agreed on the basic principles involved: our five organs of sense give us a kind of "feel" of the universe and the various things that it contains, but they do not help us to experience things as they really are. Rather the sense organs distort the reality, as if we were trying to view and understand a beautiful landscape through a camera lens that is out of focus. The great spiritual explorers who have searched for the real facts behind all appearances have told us that the universe is faultless in its conception, faultless in its purpose, and faultless in its operation. But they have pointed out that the average human has difficulty in seeing and experiencing this real universe because of his defective inner vision and his disinclination to correct it.

Penetrating deep into the mysteries of every kind of phenomena in their search for true answers, these explorers reappeared on conventional levels with tradition-shattering discoveries. And one of the most shattering of them all was this: that behind every object which the senses can identify, whether the object be human, animal, tree, mountain, plant or anything else, and right where the object seems to be, is the mental and spiritual *fact* functioning in all its completeness and perfection. This spiritual fact cannot be recognized with ordinary human eyesight but it is always apparent to clarified inner vision.

With their unclouded wisdom and their ability to define things as they truly are, these spiritual pioneers made clear-cut distinctions between the realities and unrealities of existence. From their pinnacles of discernment they recognized physical phenemena as not the real facts at all but merely counterfeits of the divine. An illusory, temporal, human concept. A mass-mesmeric distortion. "Such stuff as dreams are made on," as Shakespeare phrased it. They had various names for the inner capacity by means of which they were able to distinguish between the real and the unreal. Some of them called it "the faultless eye of Truth." Others preferred "the eye of the Soul," or "the eye of the Mind," or "the eye of the Understanding." The American Indian, with his simple, direct approach to the great verities of being, calls this valuable faculty "in-seeing," or "in-hearing," or "in-knowing."

This is the kind of faculty that I finally had to come to use with Strongheart in order to begin actually seeing and knowing him as he really was in the great over-all plan and purpose of life. My association with the merely biological part of him, while it was a most interesting experience, had been getting neither of us anywhere as intelligent and expanding expressions of life. On the contrary, it had been keeping us in those conventional and restricting ruts and routines in which humans and dogs have been moving about for centuries.

But when I began mentally getting out of these ruts and routines myself, and mentally taking Strongheart out of them, too, he and I began overflowing our banks, so to speak, and experiencing shared living the like of which I had never even heard of before. Our escape into these larger certainties began the day that I started hunting for his character qualities with the aid of the book of synonyms and the dictionary.

The more I did this the more I lifted my concept of Strongheart out of the physical and into the mental, and out of the mental into the spiritual. Thus I was constantly translating him into what he really was back of his physical appearance—an illimitable idea.

Thus with the dog's guiding help, and with him as the focal point for the experience, I was receiving priceless primary lessons in the cosmic art of seeing things as they really are—through the mists and barriers that seem to separate all of us from one another.

14. ELEVATION HOUND

WHENEVER possible, Strongheart and I would leave home early in the morning and go gypsy-footing about the California countryside, looking for fun and adventure for both of us and educational expansion for me. In these outings we observed only one rule: the democratic procedure of rotation in office. One day I would be in charge of the expedition and he would have to fit himself into my plans in every detail. The next time it would be his turn to decide where we should go and what we should do, and I would obey him as though he were the human and I the dog.

Having a salt wave ever splashing in my heart, which is the agreeable fate of those who have been brought up on an ocean-washed rocky coast, I usually headed us in the direction of the Pacific Ocean when I was chairman of the day. But while Strongheart liked beaches and salt-water swimming, he preferred open country, and the higher the open country the better he liked it. He certainly was an elevation hound.

One time as I was loading our equipment into our automobile for a trip to a distant shore line, it being my turn as manager, Strongheart began acting as though he did not want to go. I had never seen him do this before. He had something important on his mind and began trying to get it across to me by barks and pantomime. I understood that instead of going with me in the car, he wanted me to go somewhere with him without the car. I decided to turn the day over to him, which was just what he wanted me to do.

I guessed there was something in the immediate neighborhood which particularly interested him and which he wanted to share with me. Instead, he led me mile after mile through colorful back country until eventually we reached one of his favorite mountains. For awhile we both lay on the soft, warm earth, resting and recharging ourselves. Then he nosed the side of my face a number of times to let me know that the trek was about to be resumed, and we continued onward and upward.

It was rugged going. Most of the time we were completely off roads, paths and even trails, which was the way Strongheart liked to travel. But it was well worth the strenuous effort because of the scenery, the feeling of shared fellowship, and the privilege of watching the big ex-war dog in action in such terrain.

A breath-taking scene awaited us at the top of the mountain in the late afternoon. Far down below, city and town-dotted land reached to the distant Pacific Ocean, which lay as unruffled as an enormous pane of glass. Everything was saturated with color. A flaming red sun was sinking.

For some minutes Strongheart and I stood watching that splendor. Then without a word from me, he marched to a near-by ledge, sat down and resumed watching the sunset as though that were the one thing he had climbed the mountain to see. I found a spot a short distance behind him where I could sit cross-legged on the ground and watch the sunset, too. More important, I could keep an appraising eye on the big dog and everything he did.

This was not a new experience. I have said that Strongheart was an elevation hound, that when it was his turn to take charge of one of our outings he would often lead me up a hill or a mountain just as he had this time. At the top he seldom spent any time investigating the neighborhood as almost any other dog would have done. Instead, he would look for a special place for observation purposes; having found it, he would rather solemnly sit down and remain there for long periods. When he had had enough of this he would come to where I was sitting and bark me onto my feet; then down the mountain we would go in the direction of home.

Every time he put on one of these ledge-sitting sessions, I became involved in a maze of speculation. Why would a dog with his military and police background, his unusual vitality, and his fondness for action want to sit there so quietly when there were so many interesting places all around us begging to be explored? Could it be that, like us humans, he got fed up at times with the routines and restrictions of everyday living and just had to get to some elevated place where he could be above it all for awhile and mentally move in more spacious areas for a change? Did he, because of his military and police training, fancy himself on guard duty? Was he feeling like a kind of four-legged Old Man Atlas, with the problems of the whole world on his shoulders? Was he watching the moving objects below him with a scrutinizing eye, trying to decide whether they were friend or foe?

Strongheart sat on the ledge as though carved out of granite. He was motionless but intensely alert, with his ears straight up in a listening position and his eyes and nose aimed forward. For a long time I watched him and the country below, trying to discover the focal point of his interest. What could it possibly be that was able to hold his attention so completely? I decided to maneuver myself into a position where I could check what was really going on. Inch by inch I moved sitting-fashion along the ground until I reached a place where I could watch the front part of him and see his field of vision.

To my amazement, Strongheart was not watching anything *below* him at all. His gaze was focused on a point in the sky considerably above the horizon line. He was staring off into fathomless space. Out there beyond the ability of my human senses to identify what it was, *something* was holding the big dog's attention like a magnet! And it was giving him great satisfaction, great contentment, great peace of mind. That fact was not only written all over him; it was permeating the atmosphere like a perfume.

I had watched human pilgrims in such meditative poses on sacred mountains in the Orient. I wondered . . . and wondered . . . and wondered . . .

15. A DOG TALKS BACK

IN a sense we were doing a kind of tandem reverie, with Strongheart in the front position doing the steering, so to speak, and I in the rear doing my best mentally to pedal along with him in the unfamiliar direction he was taking.

Where had the dog actually gone with his thinking processes while his usually highly energetic and active physical body rested so quietly on the ledge? Strongheart was in reciprocating contact with a wise and very friendly *something;* that would have been apparent to almost any close observer; but what probably would have baffled the observer, as it certainly did me, was the exact nature and location of that *something.*

I began mentally exploring in all sorts of directions, carefully listening for intuitive whisperings and carefully following every leading. My take-off in these efforts was always from two solid facts: First, that Strongheart's real identity extended far out beyond his physical appearance. And second, that although classified as "a dog" and tagged with the limitations we humans usually hang on dogs, he was nevertheless a most intelligent thinking unit. This I had watched him prove daily as he reasoned things through for himself, arrived at his own conclusions and translated those conclusions into effective action.

"If Strongheart's identity extends beyond his biological appearance," I asked myself, "then how far out does it extend? Where are its boundaries to be placed? Strong-heart is really intelligent; millions of people throughout the world will attest to that. But who is qualified to judge the real scope of his intelligence? In order to do that, one would have to exchange points of view with Strongheart on a level of mutual understanding; only in this way could one find out what the dog mentally and spiritually knows.

With all limitations off my imagination, I began wondering if Strongheart, as he sat there on the ledge, was trying in his own way to get some kind of insight into the invisible realities back of the material appearance of things. I wondered if he were making an effort to get into the larger areas of himself, to discover more of his real selfhood, as almost any sensitive human would have been doing in the midst of such natural beauty. But I did not get anywhere with my speculations; the intellectual fog was too thick for me.

Then just for fun I decided to interview the dog ahead of me as though he were a distinguished but difficult-to-understand foreigner. I went to work on him as a reporter, talking across to him mentally in order not to disturb the sanctuary stillness in which we were both sitting, aiming all that I soundlessly said at the back of his head. I asked him questions having to do with his most intimate life, with me, with us, with human-animal relationships. There was no sequence in the questioning.

I asked whatever came to mind. I did not wait for answers; I really did not expect any.

Eventually I ran out of things to ask him. I relaxed into a pleasing feeling of suspended animation and a blank state of mind. Suddenly, and without the least sound from me to attract his attention, Strongheart swung his head around and began staring at me, and right through me, with those big eyes of his. It was unexpected—and startling.

I do not know how long he kept those x-ray eyes focused on me. It may have been only a few minutes; it may have been much longer. My situation was something like that of the fabulous monk of long ago who, you may recall, went out one unusually fine spring morning to listen to a meadow lark sing, and when he returned all his friends were gone; three hundred years had passed by. Such things as time and space disappear in the presence of greater realities.

Presently Strongheart turned his head back to its original position and calmly resumed looking off into space. And then—as easily and naturally as though such things were a regular part of everyday experience—I knew that Strongheart had been silently talking back to me. And I had actually been able to understand what he had said to me! The proof was that I had answers to practically every question I had asked, answers that were subsequently verified in every detail.

Sitting there on the ledge with his back in my direction, Strongheart had heard the questions I had mentally asked him. When I went into that blank state of mind, without knowing what I was doing I had become mentally open and receptive. Then, turning his head in my direction so as to get my full attention, he had silently answered my questions. I had spoken to Strongheart in the kind of speech which does not have to be uttered or written, and he had replied to me in the same language. Without the exchange of a sound or a gesture between us, each had perfectly understood the other. I had at last made contact with that seemingly lost universal silent language which, as those illumined ancients pointed out long ago, all life is innately equipped to speak with all life whenever minds and hearts are properly attuned.

As I followed Strongheart home that night, with our thinking and outward actions synchronized as never before and moving in conscious rhythm with the infinite Intelligence and Energy from which all things proceed, I suddenly knew why the language barriers between the dog and myself had disappeared. I had struck a right chord in universal kinship—and the rest just happened.

16. MENTAL BRIDGES

IT is not easy to make clear in words the exact technique for exchanging ideas with a dog by means of silent communication. One obstacle to an understanding is the general attitude which resists the unfamiliar, especially if it has to do with animals.

Another difficulty arises from the fact that attempting to expand one's rational relations with a dog in this manner must of necessity be a pioneering adventure. One is forced to do his own mental navigating, to arrive at his own conclusions and prove them in firsthand experience. One finds himself moving contrary to almost all conventional notions of human-animal relationships.

My greatest handicap in learning how to carry on rational silent conversation with Strongheart came from an assortment of wrong beliefs about dogs which I had absorbed from centuries of humanity's wrong thinking about them. And one of the most arrogant of these ideas was the conceit that while I, because of my "divinely bestowed superiority," was fully qualified to communicate certain important thought down to animals, the animals, because of their "divinely bestowed inferiority," were able to communicate little of real value up to me. And even when such upward communication was possible, it could only be expressed crudely and in an extremely limited way, as befitted a "dumb creature operating from a lower order of intelligence."

Strongheart knocked that nonsense out of me. Not all at once, but day by day and night by night as I trailed observantly behind him in open country or figuratively sat at his feet at home and let him quietly teach me the things I so badly needed to know in order to become a better companion for him and a better citizen of the universe. When I was willing and ready to be taught by a dog, Strongheart shared precious wisdom with me, wonderful secrets having to do with the great dog art of living abundantly and happily in the present tense regardless of circumstances.

Strongheart broke me of the bad habit of mentally looking down my nose at other living entities and other forms of life as inferior, limited or unrelated to me. He drilled this fact into me: that if I wanted to move with him in a really intelligent way, I would have to keep all my mental contacts with him as high, as horizontal and as wide open as possible. He taught me that I was always to regard him as an unconditioned fellow being rather than as "a dog" in the conventional and restricted meaning of that term.

Out of this teaching there developed a mental bridge, so to speak, between us. It was a bridge for two-way, *not* one-directional, thought traffic. A bridge extending from where I appeared to be operating as "a human" to where Strongheart seemed to be functioning as "a dog." With this invisible bridge connecting us, it was possible for my thoughts freely to cross over into his thinking areas and for his thoughts freely to cross over into mine. But there was a strict obligation in this; I had to learn never to permit anything but my best thoughts to cross our bridge in his direction; and he, I know, never allowed anything but his best thoughts to come across to me.

When I held my end of the bridge high, horizontal and as wide open to receive as to send, thought traffic flowed back and forth between us in a natural and mutually helpful way. He seldom seemed to have difficulty in understanding the thoughts I sent across to him, whether as news, suggestions, opinions, questions or expressions of appreciation. And the more diligently I applied myself to it the easier it became to understand the things he was silently saying to me.

Occasionally, however, I forgot my required part in this kinship. I elevated my end of the bridge so that the rest of it slanted down at him as though from a superior to an inferior. Whenever this happened the invisible current operating us as a unit was short-circuited, and I automatically dropped to the relatively low level of just another dumb human trying to appear important in the shadow of an intelligent dog.

Had someone come upon the dog and me sitting quietly shoulder to shoulder in some picturesque outdoor location, and had our observer been told in all seriousness that we were exchanging stimulating points of view with each other through the medium of silent talk, he would probably have found it exceedingly difficult to believe. But such would have been the truth. Had he cared to become one of us, had he been sufficiently flexible and receptive for such an experience, he could have joined in with us and shared in the simple universal language we were using, that language which moves without the need for sound from heart to heart.

What made our silent conversations so easy and so rewarding was the invisible Primary Factor that was responsible for the entire activity. In order to understand this deeply hidden secret, it is important to know that what actually went on in those communion sessions of ours was not the hit-or-miss exchange of thoughts between the "larger and more important brain of a human" and the "smaller and less important brain of a dog." Not at all. Brains as such had no more to do with it than ribs. It was *something* far more authoritative. And that *something* had all the immensity, all the power, all the intelligence, all the love of the boundless Mind of the Universe moving back of it and in it and through it.

Neither Strongheart nor I was doing any communicating as of ourselves. Neither of us was expressing himself as an original thinker or an independent source. On the contrary, we were being *communicated through* by the Mind of the Universe. We were being used as living instruments for its good pleasure. That primal, illimitable and eternal Mind was moving through me to Strongheart, and through Strongheart to me. Thus I came to know that it moves through everything everywhere in a ceaseless rhythm of harmonious kinship.

I was privileged to learn from my dog instructor how to get my human ego and intellect out of the way, how to blend my best with Strongheart's best, and how to let the Universe express itself through us, as the Universe with its wisdom and long experience well knows how to do.

17. MAGIC ALCHEMY

IT may help us to understand how the Mind of the Universe speaks through a man to his dog and through the dog to the man, if we imagine two humans who have established the same kind of bridge for two-way traffic that Strongheart and I found to be so practical and helpful.

Such an invisible bridge between two humans would indicate that they were in perfect rapport with each other, that they were in a state of real companionship. Such a state can flower only in the soil of mutual respect, admiration, appreciation, loyalty, courtesy and the mutual desire to share their best.

Thus a kind of magic alchemy takes place in which each of these humans, without sacrificing the uniqueness of his own individuality, harmonizes himself with the other so that they seem to function as a single unit. Eyes look out with eyes in a common seeing; ears hear in unison with ears; heart beats in full rhythm with heart. Their lives flow along together in integrated oneness of knowing, being and doing.

Our two humans eventually arrive at that point in mutual understanding where vocal, written or even sign language between them becomes superfluous. They find that they no longer need symbols of expression in order to share thoughts and feelings. They find themselves in perfect accord with each other; and they also find themselves moving into accord with all other living things.

This is the over-all pattern that Strongheart and I were working out together. We progressed against rather heavy odds, because of my great ignorance of such things. But the more I kept at it the easier it became. I began to see how little difference there is between mentally bridging across to a human in this manner and doing so with a dog, providing that the mental bridge across to the dog is kept as high and as horizontal as it would be in the case of an intelligent and respected human; providing also that thought traffic is allowed to flow in both directions and that the human involved has at least some understanding of the Divinity within all life which innately relates each of us to every other living thing, and every other living thing to us, in true kinship.

A number of friends had become interested in exploring the possibilities of rational correspondence between themselves and their dogs. Some of them, after much experimenting, had little to show for their efforts. They had set up bridges between themselves and their dogs, but they failed to regulate them for two-way traffic. Their bridges permitted thought traffic to flow from them to their dogs, but not from their dogs to them. They were eager senders but not eager receivers. And that automatically threw any real correspondence out of balance.

In trying to hear and understand Strongheart when he silently spoke to me, or rather when he was spoken

78

through by the Mind of the Universe, my conventional ears were great handicaps. They were geared to harsh and discordant earth sounds and were unable to pick up the delicate universal mental language, especially as it came through a dog. I made real progress only when I gave the most diligent heed to the "practically lost art of listening," which, as William Butler Yeats maintained, "is the nearest of all arts to Eternity."

Listening to Strongheart, I found, was of far greater importance than trying to make him listen to me. When my inner hearing and receiving apparatus was rightly attuned, I could always hear interesting and important things coming through him. But I lost this point of receptivity whenever I temporarily forgot that we were both living expressions of the same primal Mind and Purpose, and our relationship then sagged to conventional human-dog levels.

The most memorable of our silent talks took place out under the stars, where he and I would sit shoulder to shoulder in shared contemplation like a couple of cogitating philosophers. We would first saturate ourselves with distance. We would watch the lovely designs and purpose operating in all things, and we would wonder, and marvel, and ponder. We would listen to the Voice of Existence as it silently spoke in that language which knows no barriers of time, space or species. The magic of the Universe flowed through us, and the dog and I realized our individual and necessary places in that glorious cosmic expression.

At intervals Strongheart and I would pull in our thinking from distant spiraling and silently talk with each other on matters of mutual interest. I would ask him a specific question. When the answer came, it arrived with the gentlest kind of impact. It came as a "still small voice" whispering the needed information within . . . or a sudden awareness . . . or a revealing suggestion . . . or swift enlightenment . . . or a clear direction for solving a particular problem.

I was never conscious of having to make any particular effort in these transitions from not-knowing to knowing. I simply became as still and as receptive as possible—and listened. Sooner or later it just happened. It was like suddenly remembering something I had always known but temporarily had forgotten in the fogs and confusions of human experience.

Thus did Strongheart and I share in that silent language which the Mind of the Universe is constantly speaking through all life and for the greater good of all life. Thus did we make use of that wondrous inner route from mind to mind and from heart to heart. Thus did we cross each other's boundaries, only to find that there *were* no boundaries separating us from each other, except in the dark illusions of the human senses.

18. NUDISTS

ONE of the most useful lessons that Strongheart taught me centered around the old adage, "Thoughts are things." No one ever taught the dog that saying; nevertheless he knew a great deal about it.

I recall having been exposed to the phrase during my early schooldays and many times since without giving it more than casual interest. To me it had always seemed merely a philosophical abstraction, something to toss about vocally if the conversational winds were in that direction but nothing to take seriously in these hard-boiled, realistic and practical days.

But Strongheart, in our "dog-trains-man" educational curriculum, drove home to me the fact that thoughts really *are* things. He taught me this particular lesson speedily and indelibly, not only for my greater good as a living entity but for my protection as I moved about the earth meeting other entities.

He forced me to realize that the making and breaking instrument in all my contacts with him was my own thinking, my own state of mind, my own inner attitude. Not his thinking or his state of mind or his inner attitude —but mine. I saw that I was primarily responsible for whatever happened in our relationship, and that the responsibility lay not so much in what I said or did but in what I really was up to *mentally*.

Two facts were becoming increasingly important in the lessons: First, Strongheart and I were *mental* beings before we could possibly be objectified or material expressions of life. Therefore it was as mental beings that the dog and I had rightly to relate ourselves in order to have the rest of us rightly related, too. Whenever I worked it from this angle, Strongheart and I always moved in perfect accord. The second fact was that every least thought-thing that I sent in Strongheart's direction, whether good, bad or indifferent, almost invariably boomeranged right back at me in some corresponding outward action. This action from me and swift reaction from him were so echolike and precise that I had to be constantly on the alert, and every stranger visiting him had to be cautioned about it. Occasionally when this caution was omitted Strongheart would detect something in the mental atmosphere of the visitor that he did not like, and sometimes this collision of the unblendable human-and-dog states of mind resulted in a rough experience for the visitor.

Strongheart knew, but very few of his visitors guessed, that each of them was constantly broadcasting the real facts about himself, his thinking, his feelings and his emotions. Nothing that any of them did on the outside could possibly hide these facts from the dog or from any other alert animal. Detecting the mental inwardness of the visitors in this manner, he dealt with them accordingly. Those who got roughed up always wondered why "a great dog like Strongheart" should have treated them in such an unsocial and undeserving manner.

A most important and most embarrassing thing that my four-legged trainer drilled into me was this: No matter where I happened to be or what I am doing my mind is always much more on display than my physical body and the clothes I happen to be wearing. Neither my inner life nor his inner life nor the inner life of any other living thing is private or concealable. We are all mental nudists, always on public display for all freely to observe and evaluate.

The dog made me very watchful of my motives and very careful of the kind of thinking I diffused, especially when I was with him. And he made me do some genuine repair work on my character and conduct. There was no choice in the matter. I had to accept this personal discipline in order to keep our relationship balanced and functioning intelligently.

Practically every lesson that Strongheart taught me had to do with my mental attitude and its reaction on him, on us and on the various things we were doing or were unable to do. Accompanying each one of these lessons was the indirect but important reminder that he and almost all other animals, except those spoiled by human association, always live out from a pure heart, that is, from pure motives. He made it clear that if I wanted to get along with him or any other living thing, I must live out from a pure heart and from pure motives, too.

The more I tried to purify my thinking, my character, my purposes and my actions and to blend the best of me with the best of him in everything we did, the more the big dog and I began moving out beyond the restricting and unreal boundaries of our respective species. We found ourselves operating in the boundless realm of the mental and the spiritual, where each of us could function fully and freely as an individual state of consciousness and together as fellow states of mind in an adventure that seemed to have no frontiers whatsoever.

19. *IMPRISONED SPLENDOR*

NOW came the crowning achievement in my kinship adventure with Strongheart. He shared a fascinating secret with me, a mystery that had baffled professional dog handlers, Hollywood entertainment producers and countless thousands of his admirers all over the world. This was the mystery: What had been done with Strongheart behind the scenes so successfully to transform him from a dangerous and difficult-to-manage war dog into an understanding and friendly motion picture star? I did not get the answer to this question from Strongheart all at once but bit by bit as we shared silent talk together.

If you would understand this secret, you must first understand the distinction between *training* an animal and *educating* one. Trained animals are relatively easy to turn out. All that is required is a book of instructions, a certain amount of bluff and bluster, something to use for threatening and punishing purposes, and of course the animal. Educating an animal, on the other hand, demands keen intelligence, integrity, imagination and the gentle touch, mentally, vocally and physically.

The most significant difference between training and educating an animal, I learned from Strongheart, lies in the matter of emphasis. It depends on whether one places emphasis on the mental or the physical part of the animal. The conventional trainer, following traditional and rigid patterns, places his emphasis almost entirely on the physical. As long as his animal looks its best and obeys orders promptly, he is satisfied. This method is limiting to the animal and stereotyped in its results.

The conventional trainer starts from a negative premise. He assumes that he is working with a dumb and inferior form of life which even at its best can go only so far in intelligence and accomplishments because of its "limited brain capacity." If he happens to be working with a dog, his primary ambition is so to dominate the animal that it will be completely subservient to him, obey his every command and treat him with idolatrous attention at all times. It is as though he were constantly saying to the dog: "Now don't forget, you down there, that I am your lord and master! So follow and do everything I say, or else!"

Most of the animals that man has used to serve his own selfish ends down through the centuries have been products of this training-without-education system. A minimum of intelligence and a maximum of force are employed in order to compel blind obedience. In professional circles this is known as the "make 'em or break 'em" technique. The animal's resistance is so broken down and its spontaneity and initiative so dulled that it supinely does whatever the trainer demands. With its thinking and natural impulses walled off, it becomes a four-legged slave, submissively serving the moods and whims of the human ego that is playing God to it.

The animal *educator* does just the reverse of all this. Moving into the situation with insight and intuition, he places full emphasis on the mental rather than on the physical part of the animal. He treats it as an intelligent fellow being whose capacity for development and expression he refuses to limit in any direction. He knows that the animal's appearance, actions and accomplishments are only the outward expressions of its state of mind. He seeks to help the animal make use of its thinking faculties, so that there will be corresponding results in its looks, character and actions.

When Strongheart began his motion picture career in Hollywood he was a splendid example of both a well-trained and a well-educated dog. The training and educating had taken place on different sides of the Atlantic Ocean. In Germany he had been carefully trained into a highly efficient police and war dog, into a heavily regimented state of thinking and acting in which practically everything was planned and managed for him. When he first arrived in the United States, he was a good example of a well-trained but uneducated dog. In spite of his physical magnificence and his accomplishments and awards, he was lopsided, out of proportion, off balance. He was a long way from having the kind of development that rightfully belonged to him. A great dog in a way, he was actually a great liability unless one were planning to take part in a public or private war.

Yet out of all that lopsidedness—with the understanding and patient help of Larry Trimble—there blossomed one of the best-balanced, best-educated and most successful dogs in all history. It was not an easy achievement

87

even for Trimble. Strongheart was aggressive, set in his ways and opposed to changing his thinking and behavior patterns. His attitude toward Larry during many challenging and almost hopeless weeks of experimenting was an ever-ready-to-explode mixture of superiority, dislike, indifference and annoyance. He was constantly suspicious and watchful to see when Trimble, whom he regarded as an enemy in disguise, would start the anticipated trouble.

No command-and-compulsion efforts were used in getting Strongheart out of his militant attitudes. Trimble, with wisdom sharpened by long experience with animals, spent long periods of time alone with the big combat dog on an isolated farm, giving Strongheart all possible freedom, studying all the things he did, searching for the motivating reasons back of them, and trying to figure out what could be done to help his potential screen star into a better and more sharable sense of life.

After many weeks, Trimble found the secret by means of which Strongheart was transformed from one state of mind to another, from a belligerent war dog to a sympathetic, intelligent and co-operative movie star. Trimble discovered that deep within the big combat dog, but solidly imprisoned there, was a wealth of magnificent character qualities. Those talents and graces, buried beneath the dog's tough physical exterior, did not need to be developed but liberated. That is what Trimble proceeded to do.

The blueprint for the education of Strongheart might well have been borrowed from the famous line of Robert Browning's "Paracelsus":

Truth is within ourselves; it takes no rise
From outward things, what'er you may believe.
There is an inmost centre in us all,
Where truth abides in fulness; and around,
Wall upon wall, the gross flesh hems it in,
This perfect, clear perception—which is truth.
A baffling and perverting carnal mesh
Binds it, and makes all error: and to know
Rather consists in opening out a way
Whence the imprisoned splendour may escape,
Than in effecting entry for a light
Supposed to be without.

With penetrating perception and deft but gentle technique, Trimble began opening out all sorts of ways for Strongheart's imprisoned splendor to escape into expression. At first the expression was meager because of the newness of the experience, but then it came in spontaneous abundance. The big war dog was helped to know, to be and to share more of his real self. And it was this unrestricted sharing of his real self which enabled Strongheart to accomplish the almost incredible things he did and to achieve his unsurpassed rating in the world of entertainment.

This is the framework of the secret that Strongheart shared with me across our invisible bridge for two-way thought traffic, and Larry Trimble subsequently confirmed in every detail. But as then, so now, it is a difficult secret for the conventional-minded to grasp, contain and use in a practical way, because of its divinely motivated simplicity and naturalness.

20. RATTLESNAKES

THERE is great practical value in the art of carefully supervising one's thoughts and motives in contacts with other living things. Particularly with such creatures as rattlesnakes. These wise but little understood fellows, with their poison-brewing skill and deadly defense techniques, are experts of the first magnitude in dealing with thought emanations, especially as they come from a human.

When I first visited those parts of the West where white men and Indians frequently crossed trails with rattlesnakes, and when I had to do so myself, it was a shivery experience. I saw some of them whirl into action with their hypnotic eyes and their lightning lunges with heavily poisoned fangs. They were thorough, terrifying and deadly killers.

One day an old desert prospector, who had had rattlesnakes as neighbors for as long as he could remember, told me a surprising thing. He said that while rattlesnakes take special delight in sinking their fangs into a white man, they seldom harm an Indian. I asked him why. He did not know, and had never tried to find out.

In my travels I found that what the old prospector had

said was true. The rattlesnakes were indeed selective. They were biting the white men, and they were extending almost complete immunity to the Indians. I talked to all kinds of "snake experts," but none of them gave me a satisfying answer; certainly none gave me an answer that I would have wanted to try out on a diamond-back rattler.

Almost everywhere I went there was vicious and relentless warfare going on between white men and rattlesnakes; it was warfare to the death of either the man or the snake. But I could find no such warfare between the Indians and the rattlesnakes. There seemed to be a kind of gentlemen's agreement between them. In all my journeyings in deserts, prairies and mountains I never once saw a rattlesnake coil, either by way of defense or attack, when an Indian walked into its close vicinity.

My dog-trains-man sessions with Strongheart had shown me the trouble that unseen mental forces can cause in one's contacts with animals. And so I was able to understand why there was warfare between white men and rattlesnakes but practically none at all between the Indians and the snakes. This situation between the humans and the snakes confirmed what Strongheart had been so patiently trying to teach me: that one's thinking, in all its nakedness, always precedes him and accurately proclaims his real nature and intention. The mysterious human-rattlesnake paradox was solved for me by the teaching of a dog. The answer had to do with individual states of mind, with the kind of character atmosphere that was being diffused, with projected thought-things or forces. Almost every rattlesnake that

I watched illustrated this illuminating relationship point for me. The snakes were able to detect and correctly appraise the particular kind of thinking that was moving in their direction. Having done so, they were ready to deal either as friend or as foe with the approaching human body belonging to that thinking.

What really happens when the average white man and a rattlesnake suddenly and unexpectedly meet? Having been taught to regard all snakes as loathsome and deadly enemies with no rights whatsoever on earth, the man wants to kill every snake he sees. Something intensely emotional, savage and violent begins churning within him, filling him with repugnance, horror and alarm. At the same time all sorts of malevolent factors latent in his nature flare up and thoroughly poison his state of mind. This invisible weapon, this deadly thought-thing, he focuses upon the rattlesnake with lethal intent.

Highly sensitive to this mental attack and keenly aware of its source, the rattlesnake by rapid thought action poisons its own state of mind and turns it toward the white man with equally malicious intent. Up to this point the conflict between man and snake is mental and emotional. It is a kind of thought-vendetta, a condition of mutual ill-feeling in which each strikes at the other with destructive attitudes and intentions.

If the white man happens to have a material weapon and is able successfully to use it, he kills the snake's physical body. If, however, the snake manages to avoid the blow and gets within range, it buries its well-poisoned fangs in some part of the white man's body, and the man keeps the rendezvous with death. While the snake may victoriously jab its fangs into the white man's body, what it really strikes at is the unsocial and deadly thinking that animates the body.

Watching a real American Indian walk into the vicinity of this same rattlesnake, you would witness something entirely different. For one thing you would be unable to detect the least sign of fear or hostility in either one. As they came fairly close, you would see them pause, calmly contemplate each other for a few minutes in the friendliest fashion, then move on their respective ways again, each attending strictly to his own business and extending the same privilege to the other. During that pause between them they were in understanding communication with each other, like a big and small ship at sea exchanging friendly messages.

Could you look deep into the thinking and motives of the Indian, you would discover the simple secret of it all, for you would find that he was moving as best he knew how in conscious rhythm with what he reverently called The Big Holy, the great primary Principle of all life, which creates and animates all things and speaks wisdom through each one of them all the time. Because of this universally operating Law, the Indian was in silent and friendly communion with the big rattler not as "a snake" that had to be feared and destroyed, but as a much-admired and much-loved "younger brother" who was entitled to as much life, liberty, happiness, respect and consideration as he hoped to enjoy himself. His "younger brother" had reacted accordingly.

21. TAIL-RATTLINGS

EVEN the most dreaded of poisonous snakes is a kindly disposed fellow at heart. He wants to be understood and to understand. He makes a wise and loving companion and will always share his best whenever the human does his part in the relationship. This is no doubt hard to believe, but I have seen it proved again and again in various parts of the world with all sorts of "killer" snakes. The proof has been established by a number of unusual men and women, all of whom moved out from the same operating basis that Strongheart had taught me to observe with him: the premise that harmonious relationships are possible only after they have first been made so mentally.

One of the most interesting of these rare people was a slight and most unassuming little woman named Grace Wiley, who until the summer of 1948 made illuminating snake history at her Zoo for Happiness not far from Long Beach, California. Miss Wiley had long experience as a herpetologist and was considered one of the world's most skilled handlers of snakes with bad reputations. Indeed, the tougher, the meaner and the more venomous they were, the better she liked them. In her Zoo for

Happiness one could find almost every known kind of a snake—enormous king cobras over twenty-five feet long, Egyptian cobras, adders, copperheads, vipers, Australian black snakes, green mambas, tiger snakes, fer-de-lances, moccasins, all varieties of rattlesnakes and many others.

People came from all over to see the collection and to watch Miss Wiley handle the snakes. Visitors were permitted to handle them, too, under her watchful supervision. People also were drawn there as students to listen to her interpret the snakes from the point of view of the snakes themselves. With one of the deadly specimens nestling affectionately in her arms, she would show to fascinated audiences what spendid philosophical teachers and companions snakes can really be when given an opportunity. She would usually close these talks with the observation that deep within its heart the snake is not a troublemaker but a fine gentleman, and that when he strikes he does so because someone with evil intent has invaded his domain and cornered, frightened or hurt him.

Watching this soft-spoken little woman prove these principles with all kinds of dangerous snakes was a breath-taking experience. This phase of her work was carried on in what was known as the "gentling room," a severely bare place with a heavily built, oblong table in the exact center. Most visitors were not permitted in this room when she was gentling a snake because of the danger involved, but there was a glass arrangement in one of the doors through which the privileged few were able to watch what went on.

Watching from this safe point of vantage, one sees Miss Wiley quietly enter the room, take a position just off the far end of the table and become as motionless as the table itself. In each hand she holds an odd-looking stick about three feet long. One of these has a cuplike mesh arrangement on the end of it; this is used for stopping and pushing back the heads of striking snakes. The end of the other stick is padded with soft cloth and is known as a petting stick.

A large box with warning signs all over it is wheeled into the room and placed on the table. Loud, clattering, spine-tingling sounds coming through top and sides of the box proclaim the presence of a rattlesnake. At a nod from Miss Wiley the rear end of the box is elevated, the front part jerked off, and out into a new world of experience slides Mr. Snake. And what a snake! He is over six feet in length, beautifully designed, filled with tremendous energy and just about as deadly and menacing as they come. He is a magnificent specimen of diamond-back rattler, newly arrived from deep in the heart of Texas, where snakes grow plenty big and plenty tough.

As the snake hits the table there is a flash of movement almost too fast for the eyes to follow, the swift coiling of its body into a defense or attack position. The big fellow from Texas is set to fight anyone or anything for survival. But to his obvious astonishment and bewilderment, there is nothing to fight. There is no moving target to strike. Only the bare walls and the motionless woman facing him. The snake's head darts apprehensively in all directions, trying to discover from which direction trouble is going to come. His tail rattles furious warnings. But nothing happens. Nothing at all.

Why does Miss Wiley not do something with the sticks

in her hands? Why does the snake, with all its noise and threatenings, not take at least a practice lunge at Miss Wiley with its poison fangs?

The truth is that Miss Wiley had been doing a most important "something" to the big snake ever since it came sliding out of the box, but you could not tell she was doing it because it was entirely mental. What was really happening was not just the outward meeting of a woman and a snake; rather it was the exploratory coming together for the first time of two invisible individualities . . . of two states of mind . . . of two puzzled and wondering kinsfolk who were about to discover that they really are related in the great Plan and Purpose of Life.

From the moment that Miss Wiley first saw the big snake, she had been silently talking across to it. Outwardly she appeared to be doing nothing at all. Actually she was proving the potency and effectiveness of her favorite rule of action in all relationship contacts: that all life, regardless of its form, classification or reputation, will respond to genuine interest . . . respect . . . appreciation . . . admiration . . . affection . . . gentleness . . . courtesy . . . good manners. The big tail rattler was being lovingly showered with these qualities, undoubtedly for the first time in its experience.

Had your ears been attuned to the silent universal language of the heart, you would have heard in detail the flow of soundless good talk that was moving from Miss Wiley to the snake. Not down at it as "a lower form of life," but across to it as a fellow expression of life. And in that good talk among other things you would have

97

heard her praising the snake for its many excellent qualities, assuring it that it had absolutely nothing to fear, and reminding it again and again that it had simply come to a new home where it would always be appreciated, loved and cared for. All of this was communicated without the slightest sound or gesture from Miss Wiley.

After a while you would notice a marked change in the snake's attitude. The fast rattling of its tail was slowing down. Its head, which had been glaring in all directions at a fast, nervous tempo, was steadying itself in the direction of Miss Wiley, even though it could not clearly distinguish the motionless woman from the motionless wall behind her. The "killer" from Texas was not only feeling but actually responding to the friendly thoughts and feelings being sent in its direction.

As Miss Wiley continued her reassuring talk, but now in low, soft vocal tones, you would witness the blossoming of this unique gentling technique. You would see the big snake slowly uncoil and cautiously stretch itself the full length of the table, finally resting its head within inches of where Miss Wiley was standing. Then the first physical movement by Miss Wiley as she reached across and began gently stroking the snake's back, in the beginning with the soft-padded petting stick, and then, there being no resistance, with her two bare hands. And as you watched this almost unbelievable performance, you would have seen the snake arch its long back in catlike undulations, in order better to feel the affection-filled ministrations.

At that precise moment in the gentling process another "deadly poisonous snake" had become a member in good standing of the Zoo for Happiness. Miss Wiley had again demonstrated the fact that regardless of appearances, good is latent in every living thing, and simply needs to be called into active expression through the gracious application of respect, sympathetic understanding, gentleness and love.

22. *NAKED PONIES*

WHEN I was a boy, few pictures interested me more than those of American Indians riding their ponies at full speed through rugged Western country. I wondered how the Indians managed to stay aboard their mounts and navigate them without using bridles, saddles or blankets. I wondered why they did not slide over the animal's head or backward over its tail or off in some other way at sudden changes in speed and direction.

Later I watched American Indians ride in the famous Buffalo Bill's Wild West Show, but even at that close range it was not at all clear to me how they stayed on their mounts while rounding curves at full speed and making sudden turns. As the years rolled on I had opportunities to travel far and wide. I was privileged to see almost every type of horseman in action; but with all that experience I still could not figure out how the Indians rode their ponies with such co-ordination and rhythm without bridles or saddles.

At last I had the opportunity of meeting Indians in their own country, and of having them share with me some of the secrets of the ancient Indian art of moving in friendly identification with all life. But this secret

100

sharing did not take place until I had been put through a kind of probationary period. The Indians were penetrating in their scrutiny of my character and motives. Finally I was admitted through the invisible gate which has separated the real American Indian, with his great wealth of wisdom, from the white man. I had to learn that unless one can first walk in mental and spiritual rhythm with an Indian, he cannot really walk with him at all.

I became "inner friends" with an unusually colorful Indian chief. He was all that a man in his position is supposed to be. He was superlative in the role he played in the earth scene; under all tests he was a credit to his species, his tribe and the world he graced so unforgettably. Among the Indians he was particularly admired and respected for his moral worth and for his clear "inseeing," that is, his ability to see into causes and realities behind sense phenomena. He was also greatly esteemed for his wisdom . . . reticence . . . physical stamina . . . fearlessness . . . leadership qualities . . . and for his expertness in riding naked ponies. Astride one of those ponies and in motion, he was magnificent. Watching him ride was an experience to be grateful for.

Until I reached the point where I could talk with him in that universal speech which does not have to be uttered, communication between the chief and me had to be carried on mostly in sign language with the help of an interpreter. The chief spoke very little English by preference, and even when he spoke in his own Indian language, his words were few, carefully selected, widely spaced and discreetly guarded. He was far more interested in listening to the silent universal language which was being spoken through all things all about him all the time.

Late one afternoon as the chief, the interpreter and I sat in the lap of Mother Earth watching a lovely sunset, I asked the chief through our interpreter if he would tell me the Indian secret of riding a pony without bridle, saddle or blanket. A profound silence followed which lasted over an hour. Then a few sounds came rumbling from the chief. The interpreter turned in my direction. "The chief says that you asked a good question," he said. There was another long silence. "Is that all?" I finally asked the interpreter. He nodded.

Thereafter whenever the three of us were together I would always find some excuse for asking the chief about riding naked ponies. But I never got an answer. I did not understand this at the time; later I realized that I was on character probation.

Most unexpectedly one day, when I had forgotten to ask my favorite question, the chief wanted to know why I was interested in Indian pony riding. I told him through the interpreter that because of what the dog Strongheart had taught me about relations with animals, I was trying to learn all I could about that mysterious bond which holds all created things in inseparable and harmonious kinship. I said that I believed his pony riding secret could furnish much help for me in that direction.

For some time the three of us sat still. Then the chief began slowly intoning words in his own language, aiming them at the horizon line. When he had finished the interpreter began speaking. "The chief wants me to tell you," he said, "that for you to 'full-know' what you have asked him, you would have to be Indian born, Indian taught, and grow up with an Indian pony as your brother. Then you would understand the Great Mystery. You would be part of the Great Mystery. But he will tell you something about it in sign language and he says for you to catch what you can."

The chief held up his two rugged hands with their palms in my direction. After a pause he placed them gently together in front of his face as though in prayer. Another pause. Then his fingers came down until the tips of them rested on the backs of his hands. The two index fingers then came straight up as though they were one finger. With his hands in that position he slowly made a complete circle with them, finally stopping them in front of his face again and looking at me with a questioning expression on his face.

What I caught from his rhythmical sign language was this: When the chief held his two hands in my direction, I intuitively knew that one of them symbolized an Indian and the other a pony. When his two hands touched in front of his face, it meant friendly and understanding contact between Indian and pony. When the fingers intercrossed and came down onto the backs of his hands, it signified an interrelating of all their interests. When the two index fingers steepled up, it represented "togetherness" blending into "oneness." And when he made the complete circle with his hands in that position, it indicated that Indian and pony were functioning as a single unit in mind, heart, body and purpose. The interpreter told me that I had made "a good catch."

Whenever the chief met an animal or any other living thing, he would pause and establish mental contact with it. While the physical part of the chief walked the earth, the mental and spiritual part of him moved in boundless space, embracing all creation in a comprehensive kinship in which all things were important and all things needed in the divine Plan and Purpose. Ever helping him to understand and move in rhythm with all creation was his companion, counselor, guide and helper—The Big Holy.

The chief never reads books, magazines or newspapers; he never listens to the radio and never watches television. Whenever he wants to know the latest news, whenever he needs fresh wisdom, mental diversion, spiritual nourishment, or clearer vision about some particular problem, he goes to what he calls the Great Library; other people call it the universe. The "Volumes" he consults in this Library are the sun, the moon, the stars, the clouds, growing things, his favorite pony, and all sorts of other animate and inanimate things. He consults them with humility, receptivity and deep reverence. His rich life experience has taught him that the Author speaking through each one of these living manuscripts is The Big Holy.

23. GOLDEN THREAD

AFTER knowing the American Indian chief, I met another chief, a Bedouin of the Arabian Desert. These two men, living thousands of miles apart, would naturally be considered complete aliens. Yet they share a common vision and move in almost precisely the same mental, spiritual and physical rhythms. Their lives are held together by the same golden thread.

I wish it were possible for you, these two chiefs and me to sit cross-legged on the ground and share good talk with one another. It would be a profitable occasion, that I guarantee, but getting these two chiefs really to open up would require careful persuasion. Both talk as little as possible, finding it more to their advantage to keep wrapped in silence so that they can better hear the Voice of Existence.

We could start things rolling by asking the Bedouin chief about the world-famous Arabian horses and camels that he raises. Perhaps he would share with us the secret of how he and his animals accomplish their almost incredible mutual understanding and co-operation.

The Bedouin's gentle and modestly spoken words would reveal the reason for his success with horses and

camels. It lay, basically, in the fine quality of his thinking about them. This thinking preceded him when he moved in their direction; it continued with them while he was in their presence; it remained with them like a benediction after he left them.

His thinking expressed genuineness . . . sincerity . . . admiration . . . appreciation . . . respect . . . affection . . . a sense of fellowship in being . . . humility . . . unselfishness . . . sympathy . . . and a desire to share his best, and only his best, with his animals. The horses and camels felt the impact of this gracious thinking even before the physical part of the chief came into view.

In everything he said about his horses and camels, he gave them a mental and spiritual rating equal with his own. He regarded them as "celestial creatures," and he never spoke of one of them without in some way paying tribute to the divine qualities within it. As a result of this the horses and camels responded to him with the best they had in mind and heart, as well as with the best they could contribute in physical action.

When one of his animals is in foal, the chief takes his prayer rug and spends as much time as possible kneeling and sitting with the four-legged mother and her unborn colt. During these sessions he talks eternal verities to them; he reads the best Oriental literature to them; he recites to them from the Koran; he meditates and prays with them. Grasping the far-reaching significance of this we would come into possession of one of the most important reasons for the exceptional looks, intelligence, disposition, achievements and popularity of the chief's horses and camels.

Had we asked the chief how he acquired his extra-ordinary knowledge of animals, he would have told us that it came from the only source it could come from, that is God; that God with His infinite Wisdom, Power and Purpose pervaded the Universe; that wherever one looked he could always see God shining through all things, and hear Him speaking wisdom through all things. Then the Bedouin would have touched his palms in front of his face, whispered a brief prayer and bowed a blessing in our direction.

As we prevailed upon the American Indian chief to share some of his experiences with us, we would dis-cover how intimately interrelated these two chiefs were in the manner in which they moved with animals as rational fellow beings, as kith and kin, and as comple-mentary partners in everything they did. Also in the similar way in which each of them went about removing from their contacts with animals, every least thing that operated against shared interests . . . shared loyalties . . . shared consideration . . . and shared results.

Had we asked the Indian chief, as we did the Bedouin, how he came by his unusual relationship knowledge and the ability to make it work the way he did, we would have heard him give full credit to The Big Holy. Then with a few carefully selected nouns, accompanied by symbol pictures made in the air with his two hands, he would have assured us that when one has the "right-see" and the "all-good heart," then wherever he happens to be, he can always find The Big Holy breathing life into all things, making all things of one essence, and speaking wisdom through all things. Thus giving everything that lives not only Creator-importance, Creator-needfulness and Creator-usefulness, but making all things persons and brothers.

There is, of course, nothing original in what the Bedouin and the Indian accomplished by recognizing animals as being on mental and spiritual communicating levels with themselves. Job recommended the same practice many centuries ago:

> Ask the very beasts, and they will teach you;
> ask the wild birds—they will tell you;
> crawling creatures will instruct you,
> fish in the sea will inform you:
> for which of them all knows not that this is
> the Eternal's way,
> in whose control lies every living soul,
> and the whole life of man.[1]

Neither of our two chiefs had ever read the Bible or heard of Job. Yet each of them in widely separated parts of the world were successfully following Job's advice. The Bedouin and Indian were indeed going "to the very beasts," and "to the wild birds," and "to crawling creatures" for wisdom, reassurance and guidance in "the Eternal's Ways."

[1] Job 12:7–10 (Moffatt).

24. THE ZEPHYRS

WHENEVER I think of the great lessons that animals have taught me, I feel special gratitude to a wise little philosopher who for some time was my clandestine companion and tutor. Our friendship was clandestine because this particular fellow adventurer happened to be a skunk. Not a "home-broken" specimen but one who lived a bold and independent life of his own with great skill and success considering the general disapproval of him.

His name was Zephyr. Somewhere in the hills near by he had an undiscoverable hideaway where he could safely spend his days without being shot at. Nearly everyone in the neighborhood hated him for his nocturnal visits and feared him for the things he did to the surrounding atmosphere when they violated what he regarded as his rights as an American citizen.

Zephyr specialized in prowling around in back yards, cellars and garages in quest of food and adventure. This naturally brought him into frequent conflict with the neighbors. They often mistook him for a big cat in the darkness and used indiscreet methods in trying to evict him, thereby reaping dire results. They used almost every known method to end his career, but none of them had ever been successful. He was too smart for them with his defense and offense techniques.

My first meeting with Zephyr took place one night in my back yard. He had just knocked over the garbage container and was inspecting the contents. Hearing me, he swung around and readied himself for anything. I stood very still, as other animals had taught me, and began talking silently across to him in a friendly way. I assured him that he was welcome, and I suggested that he continue what he had been doing while I sat down on the ground and enjoyed the evening.

Not a move did he make, except with his sharp, pene-trating, calculating little eyes. But I knew what he was up to. He was adding and subtracting me. Sensing the mental atmosphere I was diffusing in his direction, he was evaluating my motives and intentions. Finally he turned around and gave his full attention to the garbage. Not once did he look back to check on what I was doing. Presumably he had heard and accepted what I had mentally said to him.

When he had finished with the garbage, he moved to within a few feet of where I was sitting and made himself comfortable. He and I removed all mind and heart barriers and relaxed. I let my mental best flow in his direction, and I could feel his mental best understand-ingly flooding back to me.

Zephyr became a regular nightly visitor. Well aware of his general unpopularity, he never came down from the hills in the daytime. He would appear at the back of the house at almost any hour between sunset and sunrise, making special code noises of his own to let me know he was there. After some weeks he began bringing Mrs. Zephyr with him; later a number of little Zephyrs came along, too.

Taking advantage of this unusual opportunity, I appointed the entire Zephyr family my teachers. We used the same educational curriculum that had been so successful with the dog Strongheart. I searched for character values in my skunk tutors and carefully studied what they did with those qualities in their moment-by-moment living.

It was a continuous revelation. I had no idea that skunks possessed such excellent qualities, such admirable moral, social and ethical codes. They functioned as a family unit without the least trace of parental or juvenile delinquency. I was full of admiration and respect for them. Their behavior expressed mutual love, consideration, understanding and confidence. They all shared a desire to help one another in all phases of living.

While my skunk adventure was going on, I accompanied a friend to a conference which had been called to take some kind of action on "the grave crisis in human relationships." There were delegates from all parts of the country. There were many speakers, and each had a specific remedy for the situation. But not one of them paid any attention to mental attitudes in the case histories they discussed. It was like suggesting various ways to paint the village pump in order to improve the village water supply.

People in the audience were called upon for remarks. I made the suggestion that in solving our relationship

111

problems we seek help outside the narrow boundaries of the human species. Then I briefly shared with them some of my experiences with animals, snakes, birds, insects and other nonhuman wise ones who had been my teachers.

After the meeting a Los Angeles lawyer, who had been one of the presiding officials, told me that while he had enjoyed the novelty of my remarks, he disagreed with my "sweeping statement" that all animals have valuable relationship wisdom to teach humans. I asked him what animal he thought did not qualify for this. "Skunks!" he exploded, following with a really bitter tirade against them. It seems he had been in a losing encounter with a skunk a few years before and had loathed them ever since. He insisted that there never had been and never could be a skunk with sufficient character and intelligence to teach anything even to the dumbest human.

I said that if I were to offer him a bounty of one dollar each for every quality of excellence that he could find in a skunk, I knew that with his ability to get at facts he would find plenty of good qualities and make a tidy sum of money for himself. He snorted politely and on that note the discussion ended; it was time for the conference dinner.

But that night (as he later told me) the suggestion of a dollar each for skunk character qualities went round and round like an insidious advertising slogan in the lawyer's sleepless mind. At his office the following morning he asked his secretary in the strictest confidence where he could find out about skunks without having to go where they were. She suggested the possibility of a book. He asked her if she believed that anyone had ever thought enough about skunks to write a book about them. She did not know, but thought it could be so. Later she returned with a number of books and magazine clippings from the public library.

Within a few days the lawyer telephoned and apologized for the uncomplimentary things he had said about skunks. "I've looked into the matter," said he, "and I've amended my opinion. As a matter of fact I know relatively few humans that I consider fit to be called skunks."

The skunks had opened up for him, as they had for me, a way to finding entirely new meanings in life and in kinship.

25. STRANGE PARTNERS

I HAVE a wonder-working friend who does most of his exploring within the walls of his chemical laboratory not far from Pasadena, California. His name is J. William Jean and he has acquired a considerable reputation not only for the many unusual and useful things he produces, but also for his ability to solve seemingly unsolvable problems for the petroleum, rubber, airplane and other great industries.

To most of his professional associates Jean is a very mysterious fellow. What makes him so is his ability to get results they themselves are unable to achieve, even when using the same formulas and equipment and, outwardly at least, doing their work in the same way.

Curious about this too I spent quite some time in my friend's laboratory, watching him work, listening to him tick mentally, and trying to find out how he was relating himself to the bacteria and other forms of microorganism with which he happened to be working. I had a very limited knowledge of chemistry and the forms of life that my friend was working with were only a few thousandths of a millimeter long, but gradually I began to penetrate the mystery and to discover his secret.

His success was established upon the following bases. The first was his firm conviction that all things, regardless of how humans are accustomed to defining and classifying them, are God's purpose in action. The second was his mental attitude toward his tiny business partners, an attitude overflowing with friendliness, admiration, respect, encouragement and limitless expectancy. The third was his ability in mind and heart to understand and co-operate with them. The fourth was the spontaneous reaction of the bacteria and his other micro-organic associates to this kind of treatment.

Seldom have I witnessed a more effective two-way functioning of the golden rule, and finding it between a human and micro-organisms was a new experience. I went back again and again to learn more about it. Here was a very wise man who had learned that the most effective way to achieve right relations with any living thing is to look for the best in it and then help that best into the fullest expression. As a result, millions of unicellular organisms, invisible to the naked eye, were turning to him with an enthusiasm that was as startling in its effectiveness as it was in its implications.

Certain attitudes and motives in Jean played an important part in his work. In spite of the stresses, strains and shocks of everyday living, Jean was carrying on in a spirit of high adventure, keen appreciation for being part of it and friendly identification with everything that lives. In spite of certain appearances to the contrary, he regarded the universe as an exceedingly well-planned, well-managed and innately good Totality. In this Totality the bacteria and other micro-organisms were included as fully co-operating fellow beings.

Jean's father was a successful construction engineer who taught his son four essentials for worth-while living. The first of these was to respect all life. The second, to be understanding and tolerant. The third, never to forget that every living thing has a particular and needed job to do in the universal Plan and Purpose. The fourth, to lend a helping hand whenever possible.

For some time Jean also was a construction engineer, employing hundreds of men on big jobs. Instead of dealing with the men in his employ as so many hired hands, he treated them all as partners. Following his father's advice, he found time to interest himself in their problems; he was alert to be helpful wherever possible, and he experienced over and over again how rewarding the golden rule can be when it is lifted above mere theory and translated into action.

One day he decided that he had finished his cycle in the construction field. Chemistry was opening a new door for him—a door leaning into regions as fascinating as they were mysterious. And so he became a research engineer, and his laboratory transformed into a kind of magic carpet on which he could fly beyond conventional boundaries in investigating the hidden workings of the greatest of all chemists, Mother Nature.

In his chemistry explorations Jean uses the same methods with his bacteria and other micro-organic associates that he did with his fellow humans when he was in the construction business. In the latter he practiced the golden rule on each project, giving his best to his fellow workers and getting the best from them. He does the same with the bacteria and other micro-organisms, using the golden rule in every detail of his work with them.

It became apparent to me, of course, that Jean was using practically the same relationship pattern with his micro-organisms that the dog Strongheart had taught me. It was the same pattern that Grace Wiley used with her poisonous snakes; the same pattern that the American Indian chief used with his naked ponies; the same pattern that the Bedouin chief used with his Arabian horses and camels.

Like all these people, Jean was making practical use of invisible bridges for friendly and helpful two-way thought traffic. Mental bridges extending from where he was functioning as an intelligent expression of life to where the bacteria and the other little fellows were functioning as intelligent expressions of life too. Intuitive bridges, built upon that speech which does not have to be uttered, across which he and the tiny ones could freely send and receive and share. Heart bridges, by means of which Jean could constantly adjust himself to them, rather than demanding that they adjust themselves to him.

As a result of all this Jean has acquired a remarkable knowledge of his invisible but highly efficient associates. He understands their attitudes toward life, their methods of doing things, their likes and dislikes and even their ambitions. He knows what they need for their well-being, their peace of mind and their fullest expression. Jean makes ideal living conditions for the bacteria, treating

117

them with as much consideration as he would human beings for whose intelligence and craftsmanship he had the highest respect. And his understanding little friends, for their part, enthusiastically contribute the best they know and the best they can do.

Out of this mutual application of the golden rule, with its rich interblending of integrity, of fellow feeling, of admiration, of loyalty, of enthusiasm, of dedicated service and of complete sharing, flow all sorts of new and useful products for the greater good of mankind.

26. WORMY WAYS

IT was a summer day in a quiet and fragrant garden in Southern California, the kind of day when the only thing worth doing is nothing at all. Two comfortable chairs were tilted back at just the right angle for dawdling and two pairs of feet were resting on a stout table. The bare feet belonged to me, those in riding boots to a friend named Axel Steen, a civil engineer, inventor, bacteriologist and authority on natural resources.

We were talking about the vast amount of generally unappreciated good that animals have contributed to us humans down through the centuries. I asked Steen what animal he considered to have been the most useful in this respect. It was a good question to toss in his direction; he has traveled far and wide, is a professionally trained observer and has a keen analytical mind.

"That's easy," said Steen, without giving the matter much consideration. "The most useful animal is the earthworm."

"The earthworm?" I said.

"Just that," he replied. "There is nothing in the animal kingdom that can top the earthworm in usefulness. As a public benefactor he is in a class by himself. If you don't believe it, come on out to the ranch and see for yourself."

A few days later I visited his foothills ranch about an hour's drive away, where I found that he had been quietly carrying on scientific experiments with earthworms for quite some time and accomplishing almost unbelievable results with them. What I saw there confirmed what he had said about earthworms. It was so humbling and broadening that I went back again and again to get better acquainted with the worms and let them teach me lessons in the art of living that have enriched my life ever since.

The only worms that I had ever known socially were those I had impaled on fish hooks or kicked out of the way to avoid stepping on them. Because of the many things I had been mistaught about them, I thoroughly disliked worms. The mere sight of them had a tendency to send me into an emotional tailspin of loathing and disgust.

Under the expert guidance of my friend Steen, however, I came intimately to know hundreds upon hundreds of these unassuming creatures and to watch them at work. Taking me into the special laboratory where he carried on most of his experiments, Steen filled his hands with worms from one of the many bins and gently placed them on freshly shoveled-up earth on top of a large table, so that I could watch them at close range.

"They're not much to look at," said Steen rather wistfully, "but if you will watch them carefully and with an open mind you will begin to see for yourself why these little fellows are such important benefactors, and why they are so essential to us humans, especially at the present time."

Steen placed more worms on the earth pile. "Until fairly recently," he continued, "the earthworm was given little credit for anything. Then came an alarming discovery: a very serious setback in crops throughout much of the country was found to be caused by the steady disappearance of earthworms from the soil. As the earthworms disappeared, so did the crops, leaving the earth barren and unproductive in spite of all the mechanical, chemical and other human efforts to revitalize it. Because of this threat of general disaster, there is something like a stampede by orchardists, farmers, ranchers and amateur and professional gardeners to get the earthworms back into the soil again."

We watched the worms that Steen had dropped on the pile of earth. They did not seem the least bit disturbed at being so suddenly taken from relatives and friends and dropped on unfamiliar territory. For a while they moved about slowly and rhythmically inspecting the terrain. Then as though they had all heard a foreman's whistle, each worm settled down right where it was and went diligently to work. I was not aware that they were at work, however, until Steen explained the situation to me. Each worm was swallowing earth in particles through its front end, grinding the particles exceedingly fine by means of an inner organ similar to a chicken gizzard, and letting out through its other end a fertile, nutritive and productive soil. They also loosened topsoil so that it could more easily absorb oxygen and moisture.

I began to understand why Steen had given earthworms such a high rating as useful citizens. And I understood for the first time why he was getting such unusual sizes and nutritive values in all the things he was raising in his experimental gardens. Once again I had come upon the example of a human reaping rich rewards by practicing the golden rule with animals, even though these animals happened to be despised little earthworms.

Steen was dealing with earthworms not only as fellow beings but as admired and dependable partners in a great enterprise. He worked on the premise that the same universal Intelligence and Energy which animates and governs one form of life also animates and governs all other forms of life. With his scientific knowledge, his experience and his ability to understand the point of view of the worms, Steen does everything he possibly can for their satisfaction and happiness. As their part in this relationship balancing, they do all his plowing and cultivating and provide him with the finest topsoil known, thus enabling him to produce exceptionally fine results in trees, fruit, vegetables and flowers.

In order that I might see another kind of their useful work, I was taken to a special observation bin which had just been filled with garbage. Steen placed quite an army of his little partners on top of the garbage. There was no confusion among the worms as they landed. They seemed to know that there was a specific job to be done, each worm knew how to do it; each went immediately to work without having to be bossed or watched. Before the day was over, those little craftsmen had taken practically all the bad odors out of the garbage, which otherwise would have become poisonous gas. Within a few weeks— I went back as often as possible to watch the marvel of it all—every particle of that garbage had been transformed into nutritive soil.

Worms are generally regarded as loathsome, repellent, groveling little objects, totally unfitted to associate with humans in any manner. Yet every one that I met socially and educationally at the Steen ranch was an inspiring example of unselfishness, industry, dedicated service, harmony and rhythm in creative action. Everything with which the worms came in contact was bettered and transformed by the experience. We humans theorize a great deal about goodness and usefulness. Those little worms were really living the qualities. And none of them taking a bow for it, either.

So if you should ever encounter me walking along a dirt road and should see me pause, lift my hat and bow in the direction of the ground, you will know that I am paying my respects to a passing earthworm. I am grateful for the privilege of occupying the same earth with such a modest, unselfish and exceedingly useful citizen.

27. ANT CODE

IFOR the first time in many years that I had lived there, my little house in Southern California had been taken over by members of the Formicordea family, commonly known as ants. I made the discovery at the close of a hot day as I went out on the back porch to get some food for that night's dinner. I had left the door of the old-fashioned icebox open. There was no ice; I had forgotten to hang out the ice sign. And milling all over the food on the inside were more ants than I had ever seen inside a house before. They were also all over the walls, floors and ceilings of both porch and kitchen. Under the back door came line upon line of reinforcements headed for the new food find.

My dinner was ruined. So was my disposition. And so were my resolutions about treating all forms of life with respect, kindness and consideration. I resented these ants in a most primitive way. Hurrying over to my nearest neighbor I borrowed a can of ant poison. With this in one hand and a broom in the other, I was ready for massacre. I was going to show those little bandits that they could not get away with pillage in my house.

I was just about to let them have it with both poison

and broom, when my New England conscience began to hiss. It demanded to know why, with all that I had been privileged to experience in relationship balancing, I should want to kill these ants. I began to reason with myself, always an excellent thing to do when one is in a combustible mood. Finally I decided not to go through with the slaughter but to confer with my unwelcome guests as Strongheart and other animals had taught me. But how to confer in a practical way with such an army of ants?

Sitting on the floor in order better to observe the situation, I tried to discover which was the head ant, or the committee of ants in charge of operations, so I could have a specific target at which to aim my remarks. But though I looked searchingly through a powerful magnifying glass, no one ant or group of them appeared to be any more important than the others. Each ant seemed to be doing its required part in the general effort without the need for direction or supervision.

Setting up an invisible bridge for two-way thought traffic between oneself and a single animal is relatively easy when one is ready for such an experience and goes about it in the right way. But establishing such an intercommunicating system with hundreds of ants all over the house was something entirely different. I decided that the only way it could be done was to turn myself into a kind of broadcasting station and talk to all of the ants at the same time. This I proceeded to do.

"Listen, ants!" I said. "We seem to be living in a topsy-turvy world. At the moment I am not entirely sure whether you or I really belong in this house. But on one

125

point I am very clear: your wants have ruined a perfectly good dinner for me. I had to go to considerable effort and expense, and all alone, too, in order to get that food for my dinner tonight. I have to eat to live just as much as you fellows do. Then without any kind of a 'May we?' you come sneaking in here and take my dinner away from me. That is neither right nor fair from any angle of approach, especially in these difficult days when we all ought to be trying to help one another."

I paused for observation purposes. The broadcast did not seem to be having the least effect on them. More ants were coming in under the back door; more were appearing on the walls and ceilings; and more appeared to be working on the food. It was discouraging; nevertheless I kept on.

"You ants may not be aware of it," I said, "but I am in a position to wipe most of you out of existence within the next few minutes with this poison and this broom. But that doesn't seem to be the right answer. We humans have been killing one another off in matters of this kind for centuries and we are worse off today than we were when it started."

Then remembering how every living thing likes to be appreciated I began sending all the complimentary things I could think of in their direction. I told them how much I admired their keen intelligence . . . their zest for living . . . their complete dedication to whatever they happened to be doing at the moment . . . their harmonious action in a common purpose . . . their ability to work together without misunderstandings or the need to be constantly told what to do.

126

I paused to take another look through the magnifying glass. The situation seemed to be worse than ever. I decided to bring the broadcast to a close.

"That's all I have to say to you ants," I said. "I have honestly done my best in this situation. The rest is up to you fellows. I am speaking to you as a gentleman to a gentleman."

I went into the living room and sat down in a chair. I felt dejected. Also I began to wonder if I were not mentally unhinged. Things did seem to be moving in that direction. I suddenly remembered that an old friend, who happens to be an authority on mental disorders, had told me a few weeks before that the line between sanity and insanity is often difficult to establish and many of us cross it daily in the things we think and say and do. Had I crossed the line in my broadcast to the ants? Was it sane to try to set up a gentleman's agreement with them? I took my confusion to a comedy theater and tried to forget the entire experience.

Returning home shortly after midnight, I went out on the back porch to see what was happening. There was not an ant in sight! Not one! The icebox door was still wide open with the inviting food inside, and there was some food on the near-by table, but not an ant in sight. I went over practically every inch of floor, wall and ceiling space in the house with a flashlight, but not one ant could I find. Those little fellows had actually kept their part in the gentleman's agreement.

This happened several years ago. Since then I have never been bothered by ants in any manner, at home or abroad. Occasionally a scout ant passes through one of the rooms on his way from outdoors to outdoors and pauses just long enough for us to exchange a friendly silent greeting with each other. There are countless hundreds of ants moving about the grounds where I live and plenty of easy entrances into the house. There is usually food that ants like in the kitchen and on the back porch. But while they invade the houses of all the neighbors and annoy them excessively, they never gang up on me any more. Our gentleman's agreement still holds good, not only with the ants that invaded my house that day but with all other ants. It is like holding an invisible honorary membership card in the Ants' Union.

28. MUSCA DOMESTICA

FREDDIE was a fly. To ordinary observation he was just a common get-the-flitgun-and-let-him-have-it housefly. The kind of creature you kill the instant you see it, not only for your own good but for the protection of your fellow man. Outside of the high rating he got from me, Freddie was utterly without social standing. Indeed, the only thing that gave him the least bit of distinction was the name that a Swedish naturalist conferred on his kind back in the eighteenth century. "Musca domestica," he called them.

My first meeting with Freddie took place early one morning in my bathroom while I was shaving. Suddenly a fly landed right in the middle of the magnifying mirror into which I was looking, creating the illusion that he was actually on the end of my nose.

Watching him somewhat cross-eyed as I shaved I began wondering why, with all the other places in the bathroom for fly landings, he had to select the middle of my mirror. I also wondered what he was thinking about. My conclusion was that, since he was in Hollywood with its high-powered pretending and show-off influences, he was posing there like an attention-seeking actor, getting a narcissistic reaction from the magnifying properties of the mirror and using me as an audience.

I got to speculating as to how it happened that such a common little nuisance as a housefly was privileged to move its body through space with such freedom, ease and delight, while I, who was supposed to be so incomparably superior, could scarcely get off the ground at all under my own horsepower except in the most ridiculous little. hops. Why were flies given the ability to walk around on walls and ceilings, and to play, meditate and even sleep on them, while I was denied the privilege?

Later while having breakfast in my little kitchen, I looked up from my newspaper and there on the edge of my plate was another Musca domestica. I wondered how the flies were getting into the house. After breakfast I went into the living room to begin the day's writing chores, and there I discovered another fly standing on top of a pile of yellow typewriting paper.

"If there are three flies in this house, that's one thing," I told myself. "But if the three flies that I have seen this morning are only one fly, that is something else."

I hurried into the bathroom, but there was no fly on the mirror. I went to the kitchen, but no fly was there. Back again to the desk, but no fly on the yellow paper. So I sat down and waited. Perhaps two minutes ticked by; then a fly appeared. He was coming from the direction of the kitchen and he was riding a shaft of sunlight like a tiny plane returning from a mission. It looked as if the three flies in the house were only one fly, and he seemed to be following me around like a lonesome little dog that was looking for understanding human company.

The little fellow circled round and round just above my head; then he dived, banked and landed again on the pile of yellow paper. For some time we looked at each other without the least outward motion but with plenty of action in our thinking areas. Then I cautiously placed a forefinger on the edge of the pile of yellow paper and, with all the friendliness I could put into it, asked him if he would not like to come aboard so we could get to know each other better. In a movement too swift for the eyes to follow he was off the paper and on my finger.

I lifted the finger to eye level and began watching him through a magnifying glass. For a few minutes he was very quiet; perhaps he was planning what to do next. Then with the quick step so characteristic of flies, he began parading up and down the full length of my finger as if he were marching to the music of an invisible brass band. Now and then he would pause and then resume his parading. He gave the impression that he was having a perfectly wonderful time and hoped I was too.

In the midst of all the swift bodily movement he stopped abruptly, swung completely around, marched to the middle of the finger and began rubbing his legs over his head, causing it to bob briskly up and down in my direction. Assuming that this could be his way of expressing appreciation, and not to be outdone in good manners in my own house, especially by a fly, I began bowing just as politely back to him. I was grateful that none of the neighbors could see me through the windows.

Curious as to what his reactions might be, I abruptly tossed the little fellow into the air. It did not disturb him in the least; in fact he seemed to like it. He cruised slowly about just above my head, but when I pointed my finger up in his direction, down he came, landing on the fingertip as though he and I had been doing such things for a long time. I did this again and again, but every time he was tossed off he would always return to the extended finger and resume his parading, posturing and head-bobbing.

As we paused after one of these landings, I slowly reached over with another finger and touched him. He skidded a little even with the extreme gentleness of the touch, but he did not take off, nor did he show the least sign of fear. I began slowly stroking the edges of his wings and silently talking across to him. Not as to "a fly" with all the limiting and condemning things that we humans usually fasten on flies, but as to an intelligent fellow being. While the world all about us was deeply bogged in misunderstanding, fear and destruction, all was exceedingly well between that little housefly and me, at least for the time being.

29. MRS. GRUNDY

AT precisely seven o'clock the following morning the little housefly was waiting for me in the middle of the shaving mirror in the bathroom.

Later he followed me into the living room like a tiny aerial dog, and while I worked at my desk he entertained himself near by. Whenever I would pause, extend my finger in his direction and invite him to come aboard, he would always do so and usually in the most artful way invite me to stroke his wings. At seven o'clock every morning thereafter and for as long as he was part of the earth scene, he would be waiting for me on the shaving mirror, and for the rest of the day we would be practically inseparable.

A few days after getting to know him I gave him the name Freddie—Freddie the Fly. I know he approved of it, because he always responded to the name whenever I called him, regardless of whether I did so mentally or vocally. We turned ourselves into a couple of experimental guinea pigs, so to speak, to see how far we could go in really understanding each other as fellow beings. There were no charts for such irregular proceedings, no co-operation, no encouragement, not even a friendly nod from those who usually understand such oddities in applied curiosity. My partner in the enterprise was "a common little housefly," and that automatically placed the entire effort completely outside practically all human approval. With the possible exception of the weather, everything was against us, but that only added more interest and zest to the adventure.

The heaviest opposition to the experiment came from the attitude of that legendary old social despot Mrs. Grundy. Mrs. Grundy, you know, disapproves of everything she does not understand, and Mrs. Grundy had formally ruled for all mankind that no one with the least bit of intelligence and self-respect would have anything whatsoever to do with a fly except to destroy the nasty little pest.

This murderous attitude comes from the conviction that humans and flies have nothing in common except birth, uncertainty, trouble and death. According to Mrs. Grundy, Freddie and I were incurable enemies engaged in a never-ending warfare in which no quarter could be asked or given, a warfare in which Freddie and his kind were constantly looking for opportunities to jab disease germs into me and my kind, while we humans were enlisted in a crusade to destroy every fly in sight, firm in the belief that the only good fly is a dead fly and the deader it is the better.

Mrs. Grundy thinks that while it may be permissible for a human to companion with certain kinds of animals, any such effort with a fly is absolutely taboo; any social gesture made in the direction of a fly, or any attempt to deal with one as an intelligent entity, is not only contrary to nature and common sense, but that any one found so doing should be turned over to the proper authorities for immediate attention.

Our venture right at the start had to face the fact of Freddie's reputation and that, I have to admit, was awful. He was, by reputation, a worthless little bum, a nuisance, an outlaw from all respectable circles, a social irritant, a disease carrier, a ruiner of human health, happiness and peace of mind.

So like all flies, Freddie lived with a constant death sentence over him. Even inside my house there was always the possibility that some friend would drop in when I was not there, and not knowing that Freddie was my special house guest, would try to kill the little fellow by way of doing himself, me, and all the rest of the world a favor. Freddie, however, was a philosopher and an artist in living. He never permitted enmity in any form to interfere in the least with the fun he was able to get out of the minutes, as he played along with them and they frolicked along with him.

One morning in the early days of our friendship, while Freddie was standing in the palm of my hand getting his wings stroked, I decided that it was high time to get a bridge for practical two-way thought traffic set up between us so that each of us could share his state of mind, as well as the beat of his heart, with the other. Such communicating bridges had worked successfully with Strongheart, with other animals, and even with an army of ants, so why not with this intelligent and lively little fly?

As I began the effort of trying to couple our minds and

hearts in this manner, I carefully reminded myself of the two basic facts that I had always found to be of the greatest importance in efforts of this kind. (1) That inherently Freddie the Fly and I as living beings were inseparable parts of an interrelated, interfunctioning and all-including Totality. (2) That neither he nor I were originating causes for anything, but instead were individual living expressions of a universal divine Cause or Mind that was ever speaking and living Itself through each of us and through everything else.

With these thoughts in the forefront of my thinking, I began silently talking across to Freddie as a fellow being, just as I had learned to do with Strongheart. I would ask the little fellow in my hand a question, and then give careful heed to all freshly arriving mental impressions, the kind of impressions or sudden intuitive knowings I had been learning to receive from animals, birds, snakes, insects and various other kinds of wisdom-sharing kinsfolk.

Unexpectedly, every question that I sent across to Freddie was followed, through the medium of these returning impressions, by a silent counterquestion. I asked Freddie what he was supposed to be doing in my world; back almost instantly came a demand to know what I really was supposed to be doing in his world. I asked him why it was that flies treated us humans so badly; right back came the question: why had we humans always treated flies so badly. Then my inner ear suddenly caught this: the important point to consider was not so much what either of us was doing in the other's world, but what each of us was doing as a contributing factor in a universe belonging to the Creator of it all.

At this point I tossed Freddie into the air and our illuminating duologue came to an end. It had to. There were visitors at the front door.

30. DECREEING

BEFORE Freddie the Fly came to live with me and made such an unforgettable place for himself in my admiration and respect, my attitude toward flies had been one of uncompromising enmity. I thoroughly disliked them for walking around on my skin, for the way they bit and otherwise plagued me, for getting on my food and for even being in the same world with me. Then along came Freddie and not only broke down this ill will but taught me things I would never have believed possible between a human and a fly.

One day an astonishing thing happened. I was sitting idly at my desk waiting for a telephone call. Freddie was standing on a near-by typewriter. Thinking of all the fun and happiness that he and I were having, I began wondering whether our experience was a kind of freak episode between a couple of freaks from our respective species or if such things were possible between all humans and all flies. Why, with the exception of Freddie, had I always had so much trouble with flies? Why did almost all humans have trouble with them?

In the midst of these speculations Freddie suddenly took off, flew toward the end of my nose, did a few loops like a tiny stunting plane and then returned to the typewriter. He did this a number of times, much after the manner of an intelligent dog trying to attract his human companion's attention to something he feels the latter should know about. So I gave him my full attention, carefully alerting myself for mental impressions.

A number of minutes ticked by on the old grandfather's clock just back of me. Then "as gently as the breath of a light whisper" a vivid impression came. All that it contained was a name and a number. The name was "Job." The number was "twenty-two." I hurried to one of the bookcases, got a copy of the Bible, and turned to the twenty-second chapter of the Book of Job.

As I reached the twenty-eighth verse of the twenty-second chapter I stopped, for there in the simple words before me was the complete answer to the human-fly relationship problem which had been baffling me. It was in fact the answer to every relationship difficulty, regardless of whether it has to do with humans, animals, snakes, insects or any other form of life.

Job, of course, was one of the all-time great mental and spiritual explorers. Almost everything in the nature of trouble that can happen to anyone happened to Job. Practically every prop that humans are accustomed to lean on for security, comfort, success and happiness went out from under him. Bitter visitations laid him exceedingly low but they could not stop him—not with what he mentally and spiritually knew.

During one of Job's particularly dark and discouraging days three of his friends—Eliphaz the Temanite, Bildad the Shuhite and Zophar the Naamathite—came "to mourn with him and to comfort him." What took place during this occasion is now a timeless classic in thinking, most of it pivoting around the challenging obligation of being in right relations.

Toward the end of this famous session, Eliphaz the Temanite let go with an observation which must have rocked Job and the others back on their heels, as it certainly rocked me back on mine when I read the twenty-eighth verse with Freddie the Fly watching the scene from my left shoulder. This is what Eliphaz said: "Thou shalt also decree a thing, and it shall be established unto thee: and the light shall shine upon thy ways."

Only twenty-one words, but in those words I had my answer not only to the human-fly situation but to every other kind of a relationship problem.

Before Freddie the Fly came to live with me, my decreeing about flies had been supplying me with a continuous harvest of disagreeable and troublesome results. I expected flies to be unfriendly, and they were. I expected them to annoy me, and they did. I expected them to bite me, and they accommodated me in that manner too. With the accuracy and precision of an echo, I had been getting back in outward experience just what I had been mentally and vocally decreeing and expecting. Since I have changed my decreeing about flies and kept it changed, I have never been bothered by flies in any part of the world, not even in fly-infested jungles.

With this discovery, I rather belatedly appointed Freddie as another of my private tutors and asked him to go to work on me in an educational way; this he proceeded to do with understanding, originality and effectiveness. Our curriculum followed the same pattern which had been so successful with the dog Strongheart and other

140

animals: I searched for fine character qualities in him with the aid of a book of synonynms and a dictionary, and then studied what he did with those qualities in his moment-by-moment living.

Freddie's teaching methods were ingenious, entertaining and instructive. One of his favorite techniques was suddenly to appear a short distance off the end of my nose and begin doing aerial acrobatics. This would divorce my attention from whatever I was doing and focus it on him, which was just what the little showman desired. Then, silently if I were alert enough to pick it up, or by some kind of physical action if necessary, he would get across to me what he felt I needed to know at the moment; getting it across to me not as "a fly," as we humans usually define and limit them, but as a fellow expression of the Mind of the Universe.

So I sat at the feet of that little fugitive from a fly-swatter, and he helped me to find and understand the real nature of a fly back of its physical appearance. And the more I was able to do this, the easier it became for us to go beyond conventional boundaries and conditions and move in understanding and harmonious accord.

Does all this seem too far-fetched and incredible for serious consideration? Then hear what one of the greatest thinking geniuses of all times has said. He is Meister Eckhart of Germany, who graced and blessed this world with his presence between the years 1260 and 1327. Said Meister Eckhart, speaking from out of the depths of his vast wisdom and vision: "When I preached in Paris, I said then—and I regard it well said—that not a man in Paris can conceive with all his learning that God is in the very meanest creatures—even in a fly."

31. CLEAN SLATE

ONE morning as Freddie was watching me shave, an idea came to me. It was this: that for me to know that my little companion existed at all, he first had to appear as an image in my individual mind. Otherwise I could not possibly be aware of him. First I must identify him as a mental image or idea, and then project that mental picture from the subjective into the objective state.

It became obvious that the instant that Freddie the Fly or any other living thing crossed the mysterious frontier between my not-knowing and my knowing, at that point he became my personal responsibility as far as defining and deciding about him was concerned. The defining and deciding could be original with me, or it could be influenced by secondhand notions. But in the final analysis all the decreeing about him had to be my own as far as my experience with him was concerned. Clearly, here was a universal law.

The first thing I did after recognizing the far-reaching significance of all this was to wash Freddie's record slate completely clean. I erased all unfavorable qualifications, all judgments having to do with him as a fly. Off went everything that I had ever heard, read or thought about

142

flies that was in the least bit restricting or unkind. It was a thorough purging. From then on it was I, not "public opinion," who did the writing on Freddie's life slate. From then on he became to me what I, and I alone, thought about him. And that sustained attitude toward my little companion opened the way for all the remarkable things which subsequently happened.

Another factor that was helpful in getting us past the blockages that have prevented humans and flies from really understanding each other was this motto: "If you would learn the secret of right relations, look only for the good, that is, the divine, in people and things, and leave all the rest to God."

Using this old precept was like waving a magic wand in all my dealings with Freddie. It transformed him into something that looked like a fly but certainly did not act like one in its companionship with me. Through the constant effort to look only for the good, Freddie became something like a character out of the pages of Hans Christian Andersen.

Maintaining our sensitive and delicate relationship was not always easy, however. It demanded that I try to understand his point of view in everything we did, and that every least thought that I sent in his direction be given the most careful editing. I found that I could allow nothing discourteous, inconsiderate or otherwise detrimental to get into my mental attitude toward him; the instant I did, our relationship went out of balance.

There was no emotionalism, or sentimentality, or wishful thinking in all this. I simply was compelled to realize that as I identified Freddie as either intelligent or unintelligent, good or bad, friendly or unfriendly, co-operative or unco-operative—that is precisely how he behaved. For Freddie was nothing more or less than the state of my own consciousness about him being made manifest in our outward experience.

When my thinking about him was on a high level, as from one gentleman to another, all our mutual affairs functioned harmoniously. When occasionally I forgot and slanted my thinking down at him in a derogatory way, down went our relationship situation too; and down it would remain until my attitude had changed for the better.

As my tutor, companion and fellow adventurer, Freddie the Fly had complete freedom of the house with full permission to do whatever he pleased. He could have taken this freedom anyway, but nevertheless I extended it to him as a mark of my admiration and respect. He was a model guest. He always knew what was expected of him and never once failed to conduct himself with thoughtfulness and consideration.

The more I was able to see beyond the physical form of Freddie the Fly, the easier it became to recognize him as a fellow expression of the Mind of the Universe. I could then listen with him as well as to him. And again I realized that all living things are individual instruments through which the Mind of the Universe thinks, speaks and acts. We are all interrelated in a common accord, a common purpose and a common good. We are members of a vast cosmic orchestra, in which each living instrument is essential to the complementary and harmonious playing of the whole.

32. SHOO FLY!

BIOLOGICALLY speaking the life of a Musca domestica is not much to brag about. Born into a world of ceaseless enmity and trouble, it goes through a few weeks of earthly existence and dies. At least that is the story as far as conventional human observation is concerned. It is advisable, however, to accept this view with the proverbial grain of salt.

Just how much actual living time Freddie had on his score board when he finally departed, I do not know, but practically all of it must have been spent within the walls of my house as my guest of honor. There was no dullness and no sag in his schedule. He had a wonderful zest for living and was able to get great happiness out of just being himself in the immediate moment.

I have told how during my training with Strongheart he and I reached the point in reciprocation where I could call to him when he was out of physical sight and he would immediately respond. The same thing now became possible between Freddie the Fly and me. If I needed him and did not know where he was, I had only to send out a mental call and within a matter of seconds he would appear. His favorite reporting place was in the air a short distance from the end of my nose where I could not possibly miss seeing him.

This soundless intercommunicating was simple after I had rid myself of inherited and educated wrong beliefs and had learned how natural and normal such things really are. What I learned from the fly was exactly what I had learned from all sorts of other "dumb creatures." I learned to stop treating them as dumb creatures.

In the quiet and shelter of our little house, where we could experiment with life just as we pleased, Freddie and I were proving the truth of the saying, "From things that differ comes the most beautiful harmony." Few things could have differed more than the little housefly and I, yet at every tick of the clock we were discovering new harmonies between us.

While I learned much about Freddie's thinking and behavior patterns, and while I was constantly improving in being able to exchange points of view with him, there was one thing that baffled me. Where did he go late afternoons after the sun had disappeared behind the Hollywood hills? I did a lot of detective work but was never able to solve the mystery. Throughout the daylight hours we were together much of the time, but when the sun made its exit Freddie made his. Then at seven o'clock the following morning he would be waiting for me on the shaving mirror in the bathroom.

One of our favorite diversions was a variation of a game called "Shoo Fly!" that the members of the famous Pen & Pencil Club of Philadelphia used to play in the back yard of their clubhouse when the sun was high in the heavens and the flies plentiful and active.

Editors, reporters, artists, musicians, actors and others would sit at a large round table, each with a lump of sugar in front of him and a supply of poker chips. At the beginning of each round of the game, a waiter, acting as master of ceremonies, would carefully inspect each lump of sugar to see that no moisture had been surreptitiously added to it by a wet finger; flies, of course, prefer damp to dry sugar. When he felt that everything was as it should be, the waiter would wave a towel and shoo the flies in all directions. Then when they were sufficiently far away, he would stop waving the towel and cordially invite them to return and help themselves to the sugar. For each fly landing on his particular lump of sugar a player was entitled to one chip from all the other players. It was social gambling in one of its most indolent and nonsensical forms.

The variation on this game that Freddie and I played was just as nonsensical, but lots of fun nevertheless. I would first mark off the palm of one of my hands into two "landing fields," with a colored crayon, one representing his side and the other mine. At the beginning of each round of the game I would get Freddie to stand on the tip of one of my fingers. Then I would suddenly toss him into the air. As he headed back I would open the marked hand for his landing, and then mark down our winnings and losses, according to which side of the line he landed on. He beat me consistently at the game, but then he was the one doing the flying and making the landings. When Freddie finally disappeared from the earth scene, I owed him over three hundred thousand

147

dollars in make-believe money. Of course, he and I played for big stakes.

When I tired of the game (he never seemed to), I would invite him to park himself within wing-stroking distance, and the pair of us would relax and quietly listen to the Voice of Existence as it silently spoke through each of us to the other. And once again the little housefly and I would experience the great truth that where there is mutual understanding, mutual courtesy, mutual respect and appreciation—there is always comradeship of life.

33. THE BRUSH-OFF

WHEREVER I went in the house Freddie would come along too and share as best he could in the activity, often riding on one of my shoulders, sometimes flying ahead of me doing acrobatics. If I were in a hurry and raced through the rooms, he would always shoot ahead and show me how little accomplished I really was in speed and agility. If I suddenly stopped he would usually make a few observation loops and return to my shoulder.

If there was something that I wanted to listen to on the radio, Freddie would stand on top of the instrument and seem to be listening too. If things had to be taken out of a bookcase or filing cabinet, he would supervise the job from some near-by point of vantage. While I was writing he would spend his time either cruising about near by or snooping around on the desk.

While Freddie had permission to do whatever he pleased, there was one social amenity that I insisted he must observe. He must not walk around on my face, hands or other exposed skin surfaces. I carefully explained to him that such walking on the human epidermis had a tendency to provoke the members of my species to violent moods and actions. He must have understood me, because not once during the time he lived with me did he violate this rule. He would walk all over my clothes, which had been declared "open territory," and he would walk along the rim of my collar and the edges of my sleeves, but not once did any of his feet touch my skin without permission.

Here was real social co-operation from "a common little housefly" who had never had any kind of schooling, who could neither read nor write, who could not ask questions, who had never gone anywhere or seen how the rest of the world lives, and who had no Emily Post to recommend behavior patterns for him. But he did not need any such human props. His was an innate ability to know, to be and to share.

Late one night after I had been in bed for several hours, there was a vigorous banging on the front door as though a police squad had arrived. It turned out to be an actor friend and he was erupting with excitement and curiosity. He had heard about Freddie the Fly at a dinner party which he had just left. He was greatly interested in the reports, but he was not willing to believe them without personal verification.

I told him it would be impossible for him to meet Freddie at that hour as I did not know where the little fellow spent the time between sunset and sunrise. I suggested that he return the following day when I could guarantee Freddie's appearance. But that was impossible; the actor was leaving for a trip to New York the following morning. He begged and pleaded for just one look at Freddie. Finally, much against my better judgment, I agreed to try to produce him.

150

The actor found a comfortable spot in the middle of a large couch where he could command a full sweep of the room. I sat in a lounging chair, the arm of which was one of Freddie's favorite spots. My friend began staring at me in the same way that people used to stare at the great magician Houdini.

I sat very still and, without the least outward hint as to what I was really doing, began sending out silent emergency calls for Freddie.

We waited, and waited, and waited. But no Freddie. Considering the high-tension nature of the actor, he was unbelievably patient. Nevertheless the atmosphere of disbelief was beginning to ooze from him. I kept the silent calls going.

Much more time elapsed, and nothing happened. Then just as I was about to call the whole thing off, a spark of highly animated life came speeding from out of the darkness of the bedroom. It was Freddie. He began flying slow circles just above my eye level.

"Is that really Freddie?" the actor gasped.

For a number of minutes we both watched the little fly as he cruised slowly about waiting to see what the plans were. Then I pointed a forefinger in his direction. Down he came, landing daintily and gracefully on the tip of the finger. The expression on the actor's face was one I am sure he had never registered before. For a while I talked vocally across to Freddie, thanking him for coming, explaining the entire situation to him, and then, as a fitting climax, introducing him to the actor.

Following this, Freddie at my suggestion landed on the arm of my chair to get his wings stroked. Profoundly

151

impressed by what he had seen, the actor left the couch and came over to play with Freddie, too. But as he stretched out his hand Freddie took off, flew to the ceiling and would not come down again until the actor had returned to the couch. Our visitor made repeated efforts, accompanied by all sorts of well-spoken words and phrases, to win Freddie's friendship. But every time he did so the little fellow would streak for the ceiling. It was a thorough social snubbing.

"But I'm not going to hurt him!" the actor exclaimed, pleading with me to act as an intermediary.

I told him that he would have to convince Freddie on that point, not me. He tried again and again, using every kind of vocal and physical technique he could think of. Freddie would have absolutely nothing to do with him.

Although outwardly polite about the situation, our visitor was deeply annoyed at Freddie's behavior. In the world of entertainment, he exhibits himself with considerable success, and he is accustomed to much respect as an unusually important person. He expects everyone to recognize this in at least some degree, and in one way or another pay tribute to it. And here a housefly, of all things, had thrown a monkey wrench into the machinery of his self-esteem. A common little housefly had given him the brush-off. He did not like it at all.

34. MORNING GLORY

OUR actor guest insisted upon knowing why his friendship offers had been turned down. We talked until the light of dawn came stealing through the front windows. As he talked, three significant straws in the wind came blowing from his direction. The first one was that he paid relatively little attention to the kind of thinking that went on back of his words and actions. Second, he had always hated flies. Third, flies had always done to him the things he had decreed about them and expected them to do.

I asked him what he would have done if Freddie had landed near him in my house and I had not been there properly to introduce them. He said that he probably would have tried to bash the life out of him as a favor to all human beings. I asked him if he thought this attitude of his could have anything to do with the manner in which Freddie had been reacting to him. He leaned back against a stack of pillows and began slowly stroking his much-photographed chin. The question had plainly sent his thoughts into unfamiliar territory, so while he attended to that, Freddie, at my invitation, flew from the arm of the chair into the palm of my hand.

At last our visitor came out of his silence. "To be quite frank with you," said he, "I don't know how to answer that last question of yours. I'm rather dizzy from what's been going on here tonight. I don't understand any of it, but whatever it is, I certainly seem to be on the wrong side. Or am I? Why is my attitude toward flies so much out of line? That's the way everyone I know, except you, thinks about them. That's the way the world at large thinks about them, too. Can a majority like that be wrong? After all, what makes this fly of yours so different from the others, except the interesting tricks that you've taught it?"

I told him I thought those were questions he should answer for himself. "But before you make the effort," I added, "there are one or two facts that I should like to translate to you on behalf of Freddie, whose silent language of the heart you have not learned to speak as yet. To begin with, Freddie wants you to understand that he knows that all those friendship offers of yours were neither genuine or sincere, that you were just putting on an act for the occasion. Because of this he does not believe in you or in the things you said to him. As far as he is concerned, you are just a common assassin."

Our visitor looked bewildered. Probably no one had ever talked to him like that before, at least not since his prefame days. I could see he was trying to figure out whether I was really serious or having fun at his expense. Before he could arrive at any definite decisions, however, I let him have it with the other barrel.

"The personality which you have cultivated and which serves you so well professionally and socially," I said to him, "may be good enough for your human contacts, but it isn't good enough for this little fly, as he has plainly shown you. When you and the fly came into visible contact with each other here tonight, he began making a swift and accurate inventory of you, not merely of your physical appearance and the sounds you were making in your throat but more particularly of the mental atmosphere you were diffusing and of the inner attitude you were projecting at him. He could feel all this as definitely as though you had touched him with your hand. And having totaled you, he doesn't want to have anything to do with you. Looking at it from his angle, can you very well blame the little fellow?"

A long silence followed. Our visitor could have been in deep meditation, asleep, or even dead. There was no observable movement in him at all. At last he opened his eyes. "No," said he slowly and with deep sincerity, "I don't blame your little friend at all for treating me as he has. I really had it coming to me."

There was another long silence. Then our visitor got up off the couch, came close to where I was sitting with Freddie in my hand and began looking at him with real interest. Freddie turned swiftly around and headed in his direction, but this time he did not take off for the ceiling. "Miracles, signs and wonders" were beginning to happen! Deep within his own being the actor had consciously struck a right chord in the harmony of universal kinship, and in the twinkling of an eye an understanding had been established between him and the fly. The actor knew this. So did Freddie. So did I. Moreover, I knew that the actor would never be bothered by flies again as

155

long as he maintained that inner chord. He never has been.

With a charm of manner that motion pictures have long recorded, the actor bowed to the little philosopher standing in my hand. "Thanks a lot, Freddie," said he. "You've taught me a great lesson here tonight, a lesson I badly needed to know. I shall not forget it, that I promise both of you." Then with a cheery "So long, for now!" he turned and walked out into the fresh new day.

Freddie and I lingered on in the morning sunshine. Thinking back over our friendship I could not recall a single instance in which the little fly had done even one of the antisocial things for which his kind are so ruthlessly hunted down and slaughtered. His character and behavior patterns would have been commendable in a human. For the fine example he was setting me as a fellow being and as a special mark of my great admiration, respect and affection, I mentally pinned a Medal of Merit on him.

Just as I was concluding my heart speech about this, Freddie suddenly took off and began flying slow circles just above my head, each circle a little higher than the one before. The sun's rays pouring in through the windows turned him into pure gold, a scintillating part of the rays themselves. Then across the centuries again I could inwardly hear the words of Meister Eckhart: "When I preached in Paris I said then—and I regard it well said—that not a man in Paris can conceive with all his learning that God is in the very meanest creatures— even in a fly."

Freddie's slow circles grew higher and higher. I wondered what he had on his mind and where he was going. Round and round he went in his golden circling. Then he became so fused with the sun's rays, so much a part of the glory of the morning itself, that it was impossible to distinguish him as a separate object. It was all one presence, one substance, one action. And somewhere in it all my little friend and teacher was being his part in the divinely motivated grandeur.

I never saw Freddie the Fly again. It was a perfect exit, by a perfect performer, after a perfect performance.